Elements of Literature

Fourth Course

Fine Art Transparencies

- Teacher's Notes
- Worksheets
- Answer Key

HOLT, RINEHART AND WINSTON

A Harcourt Education Company

Orlando • **Austin** • New York • San Diego • Toronto • London

STAFF CREDITS

Project Director: Laura Wood
Managing Editor: Marie Price
Manager of Editorial Services: Michael Neibergall
Project Editors: Juliana Koenig, Susan Kent Cakars
Writer/Editor: Ron Ottaviano
Editorial Staff: Danielle Greer, Erik Netcher, Evan Wilson
Design: *Art Director, Book Design,* Richard Metzger
Production/Manufacturing: *Senior Production Coordinator,* Belinda Barbosa Lopez; *Supervisor,* Carol Trammel; *Senior Production Manager,* Beth Prevelige

ISBN 0-03-073886-5

1 2 3 4 5 6 027 07 06 05 04 03

FINE ART TRANSPARENCIES

Analyzing ways mood is
expressed in a painting and a
poem.

Comparing and contrasting
symbols in a poem and a painting.

Comparing the mood expressed
in a painting with the mood
expressed in a poem.

Analyzing ideas in a story and a
photograph.

Comparing ideas expressed in
literature and fine art.

Recognizing how a painting
conveys a message.

USING THE FINE ART TRANSPARENCIES BOOKLET

INTRODUCTION

The Fine Art Transparencies booklet for the *Elements of Literature* series is designed to help students understand, analyze, critique, and produce visual representations. The booklet includes a series of Fine Art Lessons with teaching notes, transparencies, and worksheets that support a specific selection in the Student Edition.

Together, these components are created to address the needs of students with diverse learning styles and educational needs, including visual and auditory learners, advanced and slower-paced students, and independent and group learners.

Further, they will help students develop the following skills:

(1) Analyzing ideas and culture through works of fine art

(2) Comparing and contrasting messages in literature and poetry with visual media

(3) Evaluating persuasive visual techniques

(4) Interpreting literary characters or ideas through visual representations

(5) Describing how choices of style and elements help to represent or extend meanings

(6) Relating prior fine art knowledge to visual representations

(7) Formulating personal responses to fine art

(8) Using a variety of sources, such as books, photographs, and Web pages to communicate

(9) Creating and presenting projects such as surveys, interviews, and short plays

Fine Art Lessons

The Fine Art Lessons are designed to enhance students' appreciation and understanding of fine art throughout history and from all over the world. Each transparency is a reproduction of a piece of art not found in the Student Edition. The Fine Art Lessons include questions that relate the art to a specific literary selection and frequently to the literary standard taught in the chapter.

The Fine Art Lessons for each chapter include the following features:

- Introducing the Art includes questions about and possible responses to the art.
- Focusing on Background provides information about the artist and the art.
- Humanities Connection points out connections between the art and literature, or between the art and social or historical developments.
- Transparency acetate makes available a fine art selection suitable for viewing with an overhead projector.
- Looking at the Art provides questions on a worksheet that connect the art to the selection.
- Answer Key provides possible responses for the questions in Introducing the Art and Looking at the Art.
- Extension and Enrichment suggests writing and cross-curricular activities that extend the themes in the literary selection or art.

Collection 1 Plot and Setting • Synthesizing Sources   TEACHING NOTES **1**

ERASMUS
Hans Holbein the Younger

Using Transparency 1

This transparency will complement the selection "You want a social life, with friends" by Kenneth Koch (Student Edition, Col. 1, p. 18). To complete the Looking at the Painting blackline master, students will have to read this poem. Students should also be made aware of information in About the Art. This transparency may also be used with other selections.

Introducing the Painting

1. Is the focal point of this painting Erasmus's face or his hands? Explain your answer.

2. What techniques does Holbein use to draw attention to his subject's face? How would you describe Erasmus's expression?

3. Would you call this portrait realistic? Explain.

4. How does Holbein's use of light and color affect the mood of the painting?

5. What do you think Holbein wanted to show about Erasmus?

Focusing on Background

About the Artist The Holbeins could paint. Besides Hans Holbein the Younger (c. 1497–1543), the family included his father, Hans Holbein the Elder (c. 1465–1524); his uncle, Sigmund; and his older brother, Ambrosius.

Holbein the Younger, born in Augsburg in what is now Germany, was influenced by his father and the Augsburg painter Hans Burgkmair. After showing promise under his father's tutelage, the young Holbein moved in 1515 to Basel, Switzerland. There, Erasmus (c. 1466–1536), the brilliant Dutch humanist and a force among Basel's scholars, befriended him. Erasmus invited Holbein to illustrate his satire *Encomium Moriae (The Praise of Folly).* Other key works followed, including illustrations for Martin Luther's German translation of the Bible. During this period, Holbein's woodcuts *Dance of Death,* his painting *Dead Christ,* and his portraits of Erasmus secured his place as a master of the northern Renaissance.

In 1526, Holbein, carrying a letter of introduction from Erasmus to the noted English author Sir Thomas More, set sail for London. He met with a warm reception and stayed for two years, painting exquisite portraits, among them those of More and Sir Henry Guilford. After another residence in Basel from 1528 to 1532, he returned to England, leaving his wife and children behind. In this final English period, Holbein painted his celebrated portrait of Christine of Denmark and his monumental *French Ambassadors.* In 1536, the artist became court painter to Henry VIII. Over the next seven years Holbein created portraits of the king and his wives, working until he died of the plague in London at the age of forty-six.

About the Art This portrait of Erasmus has been acclaimed as a fine example of the artist's gift for exquisite detail. In it the great writer and scholar is rendered in an astonishingly lifelike manner. The line of the nose, the texture of the skin, and the meticulously defined wisps of hair seem almost photographic in their detail. Against his dark robe and the lavishly rendered background tapestry, the face and hands of Erasmus glow with a soft amber light that seems to emanate from his manuscript. This light can be seen as a visual metaphor for intellectual and spiritual enlightenment, since Holbein portrays Erasmus writing his commentary on the Gospel of Saint Mark.

Humanities Connection

History Born in Rotterdam in what is now the Netherlands, Erasmus became an ordained priest in the Roman Catholic Church and studied at the University of Paris. His writing, which combined vast learning with a keen wit, advocated moderation and tolerance. As a humanist, Erasmus detested the religious warfare of the time for the intolerance that it reflected and the cultural decline that it inevitably caused. Although his attacks on the abuses of the clergy and the ignorance of the laity earned him the alliance of the great religious reformer Martin Luther, Erasmus remained a lifelong Roman Catholic. The Roman Catholic Church, however, was unhappy with many of his writings and placed them on the *Index of Prohibited Books* after his death. His later critical position on the Reformation was also vehemently denounced by Martin Luther.

ELEMENTS OF LITERATURE   FOURTH COURSE   FINE ART

Collection 1 Plot and Setting • Synthesizing Sources   WORKSHEET **1**

ERASMUS
Hans Holbein the Younger

Looking at the Painting

1. Compare the mood of Holbein's portrait with that of Kenneth Koch's poem "You want a social life, with friends." Cite aspects of each work to support your answer.

_____

_____

_____

_____

2. Koch's poem divides life into three parts. Which part does the painting depict, and how does it portray the nature of that part of life?

_____

_____

_____

_____

3. Compare Holbein's portrayal of Erasmus with Koch's quick assessments of Michelangelo and Homer.

_____

_____

_____

_____

4. In his thirties, Holbein left his wife and family behind to paint portraits of England's key figures. How does that choice relate to lines 16–18 of the poem?

_____

_____

_____

_____

ERASMUS
Hans Holbein the Younger

ANSWER KEY

Introducing the Painting

1. Answers may vary. For instance, the face is the focal point because it is central and contrasted with the background; or the hands are the focal point because they are brightly lit and show the key action of a great writer at work.

2. Answers may vary. Holbein uses dark colors in the background and warm, golden light on the face to create a contrast that highlights the face. Erasmus's expression seems serious, focused, and serene.

3. Answers may vary. Students should notice and explain the highly detailed portrayal of Erasmus's facial features, skin, and hands, along with the realistic depiction of objects and fabrics in the painting.

4. Answers may vary. While the dark palette reflects the clothing, textiles, and interior designs of the period, it gives the painting a serious mood, as does Erasmus's expression; however, the light on the hands and face lends a warm mood to the work.

5. Answers may vary. Holbein may have wanted to show Erasmus's great intellect and concentration. He may also have wanted to show Erasmus writing to commemorate or record the appearance of this great writer at work on an important tract.

Looking at the Painting

1. Answers may vary. While the palette and Erasmus's serious expression give Holbein's portrait a sober, almost religious mood, Koch's poem has a light, breezy mood that comes from its playful rhyme scheme (lines 7–9) and informal language ("pictures of his Girl").

2. Answers may vary. The painting depicts work, and it seems to portray the nature of this part of life as a serious, crucial aspect of a person's existence, at least in the case of Erasmus.

3. Answers may vary. Holbein's portrayal of Erasmus is a detailed picture of a man involved in his work, whereas Koch's quick assessments of Michelangelo and Homer are superficial

responses to the artist's devotion to love and work, and the writer's diligence and socializing.

4. Answers may vary. Holbein's choice to put ambition and work before love and family contrasts sharply with the choice that the poem recounts in lines 16–18, which honestly appraises the speaker's tendency to put love and partying ahead of serious writing.

EXTENSION AND ENRICHMENT

Writing Connections

1. In *Erasmus,* Holbein shows the scholar and writer absorbed in his work. What work would you love to do? Write a poem that expresses the excitement of your dream profession. Try to capture the process or action involved in the job. Use vivid description that appeals to the senses and at least one instance of figurative language. The poem will be evaluated on the basis of the following criteria:
   * The poem expresses excitement about a profession.
   * The poem uses sensory description and at least one example of figurative language.
   * The poem is relatively free of errors in spelling, grammar, usage, and mechanics.

Crossing the Curriculum: History

2. Why is Erasmus an important historical figure? Using an encyclopedia, books in the library, and the Internet, investigate the great humanist and writer. Then, write a two-page research paper that sums up his work and his influence on European thought and religion. Include a definition of humanism and some background on life in sixteenth-century Basel, Switzerland, Erasmus's adopted hometown. The research paper will be evaluated on the basis of the following criteria:
   * The research paper sums up Erasmus's work and influence.
   * The paper provides a definition of humanism and some background on life in sixteenth-century Basel.
   * The paper is relatively free of errors in spelling, grammar, usage, and mechanics.

POSTER FOR RINGLING BROS. AND BARNUM & BAILEY CIRCUS

Using Transparency 2

Use this transparency with "The Leap" by Louise Erdrich (Student Edition, Col. 1, p. 31). To complete the Looking at the Poster blackline master, students will have to read this short story. Students should also be made aware of information in About the Art. This transparency may also be used with other selections.

Introducing the Poster

1. What acts, either parading or performing, are shown in this circus poster? How many rings (or different performing areas) do you count under the big top?

2. What are the dominant colors in the poster? What mood do these colors convey?

3. Why do you think the artist chose not to have a center of interest or focal point in the poster?

4. Does looking at this poster make you want to go to the circus? Why or why not?

5. Do you think the written information on the poster is useful and effective? Why or why not?

Focusing on Background

About the Art Since the mid-1800s, colorful posters publicizing a circus's visit to town have been as much a part of circuses as showy costumes and brass bands. Each circus had a publicity team that went ahead on the tour route and put up posters to create excitement for the coming show. This 1928 poster advertises an appearance of the Ringling Bros. and Barnum & Bailey Circus Combined Shows. Some of the Ringling–Barnum posters urged the public to bypass lesser circuses and "wait for the big show."

The name *Ringling Bros. and Barnum & Bailey Circus* is famous throughout the world. The merger of three circuses over time led to the creation of the lengthy but magical name and to history's largest and most famous circus. P. T. Barnum (1810–1891), the legendary showman from Connecticut, and two partners began Barnum's circus in 1871, which was around the beginning of a time of great popularity for circuses in the United States. Barnum's circus crossed the country in as many as seventy railroad cars rather than in the traditional horse-drawn wagons. James A. Bailey's circus joined with Barnum's in 1881. The following year Barnum added Jumbo, an African elephant from the London Zoo, to his circus cast. In 1888, Barnum & Bailey's circus was billed as "The Greatest Show on Earth" and was then the biggest circus.

Meanwhile, the Ringling brothers were developing a traveling circus of their own that would rival and eventually purchase Barnum & Bailey's. The Ringling brothers were first-generation Americans; their father, a harness maker, was from Germany. Five Ringling brothers—Albert, Otto, Alfred, Charles, and John—opened their traveling circus in 1884 in Wisconsin. The brothers and seventeen employees did all the work, including performing, playing in the band, selling tickets, and pitching the tents. Henry and August Ringling later joined their brothers. Each brother managed a different aspect of the circus. The Ringlings prospered and in 1907 bought the Barnum & Bailey circus. The two circuses toured independently, however, until 1919, when they officially became the Ringling Bros. and Barnum & Bailey Circus. The new circus was presented under a giant tent, known as the big top, until 1956; since that time it has been presented in indoor arenas. In 1967, the Ringling family sold the circus.

Humanities Connection

Daily Life For performers in the Ringling Bros. and Barnum & Bailey Circus, railroad coach cars are home for about ten and a half months of the year. Each of the circus's two units has its own train and travels about 25,000 miles a year in the United States and Canada. When not traveling, circus performers are preparing for the next season at Ringling's winter quarters in Venice, Florida. There they live in houses or mobile homes.

NAME _____ CLASS _____ DATE _____

POSTER FOR RINGLING BROS. AND BARNUM & BAILEY CIRCUS

Looking at the Poster

1. What details in the poster evoke the **setting** of the fateful first leap in Louise Erdrich's "The Leap"?

2. Compare the mood of the poster with that of the story, and explain how the purpose of each work determines its mood.

3. How do the subject matter and color of the poster evoke the **climax** of Erdrich's **plot**?

4. In "The Leap," the narrator thinks her mother's "catlike precision . . . might be the result of her early training." Investigate the story's setting, and explain whether that training may have taken place when this poster was produced.

Fine Art Transparencies

POSTER FOR RINGLING BROS. AND BARNUM & BAILEY CIRCUS

ANSWER KEY

Introducing the Poster

1. The poster shows horse, elephant, clown, balancing, and acrobatic acts. Six rings are visible.

2. The dominant colors are red, orange, yellow, and green. These colors create a lively, exciting mood.

3. Answers may vary. The lack of a focal point emphasizes the variety and excitement of the circus and the fact that spectators have many acts to watch at the same time.

4. Answers may vary. Most students probably will say that the colorful, exciting depictions of the circus performers make the circus look inviting. Others may find all the activity too stimulating or quaint and would not want to attend.

5. Answers may vary. Most students probably will think that the information is useful and effective because it states the name of the show; emphasizes that people will see not just one, but two, shows ("combined shows"); and intrigues the viewer by advertising the acts' quality ("greatest") and diversity ("from every country in the world").

Looking at the Poster

1. Poster details that evoke the story's first leap include the tumbling and flying acrobats and trapeze artists, the circus big tent, the poles, and the audience.

2. The mood of the poster is vibrant and exciting, whereas the story's mood is wistful, thoughtful, even sad. The poster's purpose is to convince people to go to the circus, whereas the story's purpose is to express deep and complex feelings of love, gratitude, and sadness.

3. Answers may vary. The poster's subject matter of leaping acrobats, general pandemonium, and rapt onlookers and its vibrant flamelike colors

evoke, respectively, the narrator's mother's brave leap, the chaos. the crowd, and the fire in the story's climax.

4. Answers may vary. The story's thirteenth paragraph, which recounts how the narrator's mother and father met, seems to take place shortly after the end of World War II. Since the mother, Anna, is probably twenty-five to thirty at the time (1945–1950), it's possible she may have been learning trapeze artistry as a young girl in the late 1920s.

EXTENSION AND ENRICHMENT

Writing Connections

1. Write a poem in blank verse about some aspect of circus performing portrayed in the poster. Your poem may be lighthearted or serious. The poem will be evaluated on the basis of the following criteria:
   • The subject of the poem is derived from images in the circus poster.
   • The poem is written in blank verse.
   • The poem is relatively free of errors in spelling.

Crossing the Curriculum: History

2. Use books, encyclopedias, the Internet, or other reference sources to research the origin of circuses. What were the first circuses like? To what types of audiences did they appeal? After taking careful notes, write two to three paragraphs summarizing what you have learned. The report will be evaluated on the basis of the following criteria:
   • The report accurately summarizes the information obtained from reference sources.
   • The report gives specific answers to the questions in the assignment.
   • The report is relatively free of errors in spelling, grammar, usage, and mechanics.

#4 THE SUNFLOWERS QUILTING BEE AT ARLES
Faith Ringgold

Using Transparency 3

Use this transparency with "Everyday Use" by Alice Walker (Student Edition, Col. 2, p. 76). To complete the Looking at the Story Quilt blackline master, students will have to read this short story. Students should also be made aware of information in About the Art. This transparency may also be used with other selections.

Introducing the Story Quilt

1. What is the setting of this scene? Describe what you see.

2. How does the artist's use of color affect the mood of the work?

3. What might the sunflowers symbolize to Ringgold?

4. The people Ringgold depicts are famous. Do you recognize any of them? What might the women have in common besides their race?

5. What do you think Ringgold was trying to express in this work of art?

Focusing on Background

About the Artist When she was a baby in the early 1930s, Faith Ringgold's mother pushed her, wrapped in a colorful, handmade quilt, in a buggy through New York City's Harlem. Memories of that quilt stayed with the artist. As a young girl, Ringgold had sewing lessons from her mother, a fashion designer. Years later, Ringgold, already an established painter, began shaping works of art using quilting and stitching techniques handed down in her family for generations.

Echoes of Harlem was Ringgold's first painting using the quilt medium. It was made in 1980 with her mother. The next year her mother died, and the artist began creating quilt paintings in her honor. In 1983, Ringgold's quilted paintings led to her invention of story quilts, which contain written stories in addition to the usual visual images and patterns. Her first story quilt was *Who's Afraid of Aunt Jemima?* Another story quilt, *Tar Beach,* led in 1991 to her first picture book, which won the prestigious Caldecott award for children's literature.

Ringgold is a professor of art at the University of California in San Diego. She has B.S. and M.A. degrees in visual art from the City College of New York. Ringgold's art, in addition to its appearance in many successful shows, adorns the permanent collections of important museums such as the Studio Museum of Harlem, the Museum of Modern Art, and the Metropolitan Museum of Art.

About the Art Faith Ringgold created the story quilt *#4 The Sunflowers Quilting Bee at Arles* in 1991. The quilt uses acrylic paint and pieced fabric and is one of twelve story quilts in a series known as the French Collection, for which Ringgold gathered ideas in France. In the stories written on the art, Ringgold chronicles the life of a fictional but somewhat autobiographical woman named Willia Marie Simone.

In this story quilt, Willia has discovered the National Sunflower Quilters Society of America meeting in Arles, a city in southeast France. The Dutch painter Vincent van Gogh (1853–1890) adored sunny Arles and lived there for over a year, creating some two hundred paintings, including his masterpiece *Sunflowers* (1888). Working on a quilt of sunflowers are eight African American women who have been important to the civil rights movement. Seated from left to right are businesswoman Maggie L. Walker, social reformer Sojourner Truth, journalist Ida B. Wells-Barnett, civil rights activist Fannie Lou Hamer, abolitionist Harriet Tubman, civil rights activist Rosa Parks, educator Mary McLeod Bethune, and civil rights activist Ella Baker. Also pictured is van Gogh, holding the vase with his famous sunflowers. The work reflects the focus of Ringgold's art—the African American experience—while acknowledging the influence of European art on the work of American artists.

Humanities Connection

Daily Life In preindustrial America, quilting was a social as well as a useful activity. People, usually women, traded scraps of material and quilt patterns. The patterns traveled across the country with settlers and were printed in newspapers and farmers' journals. Favorite patterns included Double Wedding Ring and Dutch Doll. Quilting bees (parties) were popular. It became a custom for grandmothers to make quilts for their grandchildren.

Collection 2 Character • Using Primary and Secondary Sources   WORKSHEET **3**

#4 THE SUNFLOWERS QUILTING BEE AT ARLES
Faith Ringgold
Looking at the Story Quilt

1. How does Ringgold's story quilt relate to Alice Walker's story "Everyday Use"?

_____

_____

_____

_____

2. How does Walker's Wangero (Dee) **character** reflect the ideas Ringgold addresses in her art?

_____

_____

_____

_____

3. Look at Ringgold's sunflowers. How might they echo and symbolize the women in the painting? What character might they symbolize in "Everyday Use"?

_____

_____

_____

_____

4. Compare how Ringgold's visual style and imagery and Walker's prose style and imagery look to folk traditions to chronicle black history.

_____

_____

_____

_____

#4 THE SUNFLOWERS QUILTING BEE AT ARLES
Faith Ringgold

ANSWER KEY

Introducing the Story Quilt

1. Answers may vary. The setting is a sunflower field near a town that has colorful, multistoried buildings. The sky is clear and blue, and the trees are full and green.

2. Answers may vary. Ringgold's use of bright, strong colors gives the work a happy, upbeat mood.

3. Answers may vary. The sunflowers may symbolize art, joy, beauty, or the harmony in nature.

4. Answers may vary. Sojourner Truth and Harriet Tubman may be the most familiar to students; they may also recognize Vincent van Gogh. Students may correctly conclude that the women have all been involved in obtaining civil rights for African Americans.

5. Answers may vary. In addition to honoring the vibrance and creativity of African American women, Ringgold may have wanted to show their teamwork in bringing beauty to everyday objects, their efforts to keep traditions alive, and their work in the civil rights struggle.

Looking at the Story Quilt

1. Answers may vary. Both works use a quilt as a central image, and both works are concerned with the strength and vibrance of African American women.

2. Answers may vary. The Wangero character, despite her perhaps selfish ways, views African American quilts and quiltmaking as art worthy of display, as opposed to everyday use. The view reflects Ringgold's ideas in that the artist clearly incorporates the tradition of African American quiltmaking in her art.

3. Answers may vary. The sunflowers may symbolize the women she portrays since she paints the center, or face, of the sunflowers (with the exception of those van Gogh is holding) with the same color she uses for the faces of most of the women. Most students will probably say the

sunflowers could symbolize the mother character in "Everyday Use" since she is the family's quiltmaker.

4. Answers may vary. Ringgold's visual style highlights the African American folk tradition by setting her painting on top of a quilt, which suggests that the tradition is the basis of her work, and by painting in a folk art style a picture of great women in black history as quiltmakers. Walker's prose style, both in narration and dialogue, uses the diction of common African American usage and the imagery of ancestral quilts to chronicle the black history of "everyday," or uncelebrated, people.

EXTENSION AND ENRICHMENT

Writing Connections

1. Choose two of the famous women in Faith Ringgold's story quilt and learn about them in encyclopedias, books, the Internet, or other sources. Then, use your knowledge of the women and your imagination to write a conversation that they could be having while quilting. The dialogue will be evaluated on the basis of the following criteria:
   • The dialogue shows a familiarity with the lives of the two women conversing.
   • The personalities of the two women are revealed through their speech.
   • The dialogue is relatively free of errors in spelling, grammar, usage, and mechanics, except for features of dialect.

Crossing the Curriculum: Art

2. Design a quilt. On a blank sheet of paper, draw the design for your quilt in color. Be sure to include dotted black lines to indicate how you would make the stitching on it. Your design should reflect an aspect of your heritage or your own interests. The quilt design will be evaluated on the basis of the following criteria:
   • The design is original and reflects the artist's heritage or interests.
   • The stitching marks are part of the design.

GRRRRRRRRRRR!!
Roy Lichtenstein

Using Transparency 4

This transparency will complement the selection "The Storyteller" by Saki (Student Edition, Col. 3, p. 154). To complete the Looking at the Painting blackline master, students will have to read this story. Students should also be made aware of information in About the Art. This transparency may also be used with other selections.

Introducing the Painting

1. What elements of Lichtenstein's painting remind you of comic books or comic strips?

2. How is black used in the painting?

3. What effect do Lichtenstein's blue dots (called Benday dots) have on the work?

4. Look at the painting carefully. What part of it do you find the most striking? Explain your answer.

5. Do you consider *Grrrrrrrrrr!!* a serious artwork? What ideas do you think Lichtenstein intended to express? Explain your answers.

Focusing on Background

About the Artist "One of the purposes of my painting," Roy Lichtenstein (1923–1997) said, "is to counter liking what you're familiar with." Whether it's with comics or abstract brush strokes, his work raises issues of the appropriation of the work of other artists, the representation of three dimensions on a flat plane, and notions of what art is.

Lichtenstein, born in New York City, described his middle-class childhood as uneventful. In his senior year of high school, being interested in painting, he enrolled in the Art Students League, studying with Reginald Marsh and painting street scenes and jazz musicians. After high school he enrolled at Ohio State University's School of Fine Arts, but in 1943 World War II interrupted his studies. He served in Europe until 1946 and then returned to Ohio State, where he received his bachelor's degree, followed by his master's.

After supporting his family as an engineering draftsman for years, Lichtenstein got a teaching job at the State University of New York at Oswego in 1957. By then his work used loosely drawn cartoon

figures. In 1961, Lichtenstein started making paintings entirely of comic-strip figures, introducing his word balloons, bold black outlines, and Benday-dot grounds (main surfaces). In 1962, the Leo Castelli Gallery in New York began showing his work, which caused an instant stir. By the mid-1960s, with conceptual mischief, the artist was applying his pop-conceptual approach to landscapes, product packaging, even re-creations of famous paintings. By the mid-1970s, he took on the subject of artistic style, playing with aspects of art movements.

About the Art Funny and deceptively smart, *Grrrrrrrrrr!!* shows signature facets of the style of Lichtenstein. Imitating the graphic and text elements of comics, he offers a pop-art image of a scary dog with cartoon-black lines. Hot yellow, used for synthetic land, sets off a sky of blue Benday dots, Lichtenstein's reference to a low-cost process used to print color images on newspaper. To get this effect, the artist magnified his drawings and projected them onto canvas. He then colored in the dots by hand. Though he used brushes, Lichtenstein said he wanted his work to have "an unartistic style, as artificial as possible." With irony, the work also comments on a society that the artist saw as "pervaded by junk." Yet Lichtenstein's big, angry dog carries enough symbolic weight to stir a viewer's emotions. If we look closely, though, we see that his dog has human eyes with arched brows that, while fierce, seem as ironic as the artist himself.

Humanities Connection

History The modern comic strips from which Lichtenstein drew are about as old as movies. In the late 1800s, illustrators sought new means of graphic communication. At the same time print technology improved, aiding the development of the new medium. Words in early comics arose in the 1870s. A pioneer of the form was Angelo Agostini, a Brazilian. But Richard Fenton Outcalt's *The Yellow Kid,* in 1896, is considered the first comic strip. While Outcalt synthesized earlier techniques, he introduced two new ones: word balloons and a series of panels.

Collection 3 Narrator and Voice • Generating Research Questions WORSHEET **4**

GRRRRRRRRRRR!!
Roy Lichtenstein

Looking at the Painting

1. How does Lichtenstein's portrayal of the dog differ from the description of the wolf in Saki's story "The Storyteller"? How is it similar?

_____

_____

_____

_____

2. How does the image in this painting relate to the theme of the story?

_____

_____

_____

_____

3. Compare the mood of Lichtenstein's painting with the mood of Saki's story. Cite aspects of each work to support your answer.

_____

_____

_____

_____

4. *Grrrrrrrrrrr!!* is conceptual: It is about ideas that comment on life or society. How is the "voice" behind Lichtenstein's ideas like the **narrator's voice** in Saki's story?

_____

_____

_____

_____

GRRRRRRRRRRR!!
Roy Lichtenstein

ANSWER KEY

Introducing the Painting

1. Answers may vary. Elements of comic books and comic strips include the style of illustration, the bold black outlines and shadowing, the big stylized caption, and the little blue dots.

2. Answers may vary. Black is used to form the outline of the dog, the letters, and the contour of the yellow ground; it also indicates areas of shadow on the dog, providing a sharp contrast to the pure white of the dog's body.

3. Answers may vary. The blue Benday dots suggest an image printed on paper in an automated process, and they also give the idea that this picture has been magnified because these dots are usually not visible in print images.

4. Answers may vary. Although some students may find the yellow ground or zany caption the most striking element in the painting, most will probably choose the dog's expression, particularly the eyes, as the most arresting part of the image.

5. Answers may vary. Some students may see the work as having comical and posterlike characteristics not usually associated with serious artwork, whereas others may argue for the validity of pop-art imagery. Lichtenstein intended viewers to examine the nature and extent of pop images in modern life and the contradictions involved in expressing three dimensions on a flat surface.

Looking at the Painting

1. Answers may vary. Lichtenstein's portrayal of the dog differs from the description of the wolf in "The Storyteller" in that the dog is cartoon-like and not colored in, but the wolf is described as "mud-colored . . . with a black tongue and pale green eyes." It is similar in that, like the wolf, the dog is portrayed as ferocious.

2. Answers may vary. The image, in a sense, refers to ferocious dogs and wolves seen in old fairy tales such as "Little Red Riding Hood," which are at some level scary, brutal stories. The theme of "The Storyteller," and perhaps an idea

in Lichtenstein's painting, is that people are naturally fascinated by things that are frightening and gruesome.

3. Answers may vary. Most students will probably find the mood of both the painting and the story light and comic.

4. Answers may vary. The "voice" behind Lichtenstein's ideas—that pop, or throwaway, imagery is worthy subject matter for fine art and that our society is "pervaded by junk"—has a witty, ironic tone, which is the tone of the narrator's voice in "The Storyteller."

EXTENSION AND ENRICHMENT

Writing Connections

1. Illustrate and write a comic strip about a dog. It can be funny, suspenseful, even crazy, but the story should have a beginning, a middle, and an ending. Create at least one other character besides your dog, and try to give each character a distinct personality. The strip should use word balloons to express the interaction of the characters. The comic strip will be evaluated on the basis of the following criteria:
   • The comic strip has at least two characters, including the dog, and a story with a beginning, a middle, and an ending.
   • The comic strip has at least six panels and uses word balloons.
   • The comic strip is relatively free of errors in spelling, grammar, usage, and mechanics.

Crossing the Curriculum: Art / Communication

2. Make a pop-art illustration of a mass-culture subject, and then incorporate text to advertise the subject. Use eye-catching colors and crisp outlines, and write text that advertises your subject. The illustration will be evaluated on the basis of the following criteria:
   • The illustration is eye-catching and fairly neat.
   • The text effectively advertises the subject.
   • The text is relatively free of errors in spelling, grammar, usage, and mechanics.

FLOATING CITY
Robert McCall

Using Transparency 5

Use this transparency with "The Cold Equations" by Tom Godwin (Student Edition, Col. 3, p. 163). To complete the Looking at the Painting blackline master, students will have to read this short story. Students should also be made aware of information in About the Art. This transparency may also be used with other selections.

Introducing the Painting

1. What are some prominent features of McCall's floating city?

2. This painting is futuristic, but are its details realistic? Why or why not?

3. What are the dominant colors in *Floating City*? Would you say that the palette is "cool" or "warm"?

4. Why might the artist have painted this floating city?

5. What value do you think the artist places on imagination?

Focusing on Background

About the Artist Painter Robert McCall rocketed to fame along with the American space program in the 1960s. With his brushes and paints, McCall has been chronicling astronauts and rockets almost as long as the National Aeronautics and Space Administration (NASA) has been preparing space missions.

McCall was born in Columbus, Ohio, in 1919. As a boy, he enjoyed reading magazines about science fiction, science, technology, and exploration. He also liked to draw and was interested in flying machines. He attended Columbus Fine Art School, and afterward illustrated articles, often about aviation, for such magazines as *Life* and *Popular Science*.

As American space exploration progressed, McCall was one of the first artists invited to paint NASA activities and over the years has become the country's most famous "space" artist. One of his best-known works is the six-story mural about the moon landing that is in the National Air and Space Museum in Washington, D.C. McCall has also designed stamps depicting the space program for the U.S. Postal Service. His stamp designs have included images from the *Pioneer, Skylab, Apollo,* and *Apollo-Soyuz* missions; the *Viking* spacecraft on Mars; and many shuttle missions.

About the Art This painting is part of a series depicting what Robert McCall terms "floating cities." In the series, begun in 1971, McCall shows versions of futuristic cities that are not tied to gravity and therefore can move freely above the earth's surface. This view of a floating city is representative of the vivid imagination and attention to detail that McCall brings to his futuristic scenes.

McCall said that his aim in doing the series was to paint a realistic scene that would capture people's attention and make them think about some of the possibilities of the future. McCall not only paints a bright future for the earth but also believes in one as well. As this painting indicates, McCall has confidence that, based on what humankind has already achieved in science, technology, and the space program, the people of the future will create improved cities and environments in which to live.

The artist began painting futuristic scenes in the 1960s. After imagining spacecraft of the future for a *Life* magazine article, McCall painted posters to advertise Stanley Kubrick's film *2001: A Space Odyssey.* He became excited about imagining an abundant future filled with new kinds of technology, vehicles, and environments. He has contributed art for *Star Trek* movies and for *The Black Hole.*

Humanities Connection

Science and Technology Developing new space technology and aviation, as well as exploring space, are the broad responsibilities of the National Aeronautics and Space Administration (NASA), created by the National Aeronautics and Space Act of 1958. An independent civilian agency of the U.S. government, NASA experienced tremendous growth in the 1960s with its 25-billion-dollar program to put a person on the moon. At one point in the program, more than 400,000 people were working on the moon project.

Collection 3 Narrator and Voice • Generating Research Questions   WORKSHEET **5**

FLOATING CITY
Robert McCall

Looking at the Painting

1. How does the mood of McCall's painting compare with the mood of Tom Godwin's science fiction story "The Cold Equations"?

_____

_____

_____

_____

2. Compare the floating city with the *Stardust* and the EDS in "The Cold Equations."

_____

_____

_____

_____

3. By choosing a distanced view of his floating city, how does McCall's approach to his subject differ from Godwin's?

_____

_____

_____

_____

4. Considering McCall's palette and scenic details, how does his voice contrast with Godwin's **narrator's voice**? How do McCall's and Godwin's views of technology differ?

_____

_____

_____

_____

FLOATING CITY
Robert McCall

ANSWER KEY

Introducing the Painting

1. Answers will vary. Prominent features include various towers, legs, flags, decks, domes, turrets, and lights.

2. Answers may vary. Most students probably will think that the details are realistic because McCall's depictions of the crafts and the background, especially the clouds and mountains, look as if they could be real. Some students may note, however, that the details are somewhat blurred and impressionistic and therefore may not consider them completely realistic.

3. The dominant colors are various blues (most of which are deep), violets, off-whites, and grays. This palette is cool.

4. Answers may vary. McCall may have wanted to communicate his belief in a bright future that included technological and aviation marvels.

5. Answers may vary. The artist of such an imaginative scene of the future would surely value and encourage the use of imagination.

Looking at the Painting

1. Answers may vary. The mood of McCall's painting is cool, quiet, and serene, while the mood of Godwin's short story is cold, hard, suspenseful, and sad.

2. Answers may vary. The floating city appears to be a large, self-contained space vehicle. The *Stardust* is a complex cruiser, powered by nuclear converters, that may be as big or bigger than a floating city. The EDS is much smaller than a floating city or a cruiser. It is a collapsible dispatch ship that is carried aboard a cruiser and powered by rocket drive.

3. Answers may vary. McCall's approach differs from Godwin's in that the artist's remove highlights the fascinating technology and architecture of his floating city while precluding a look at the human beings who live in it. Godwin's approach focuses intently on the lives of the people, or characters, who are traveling in his space cruiser *Stardust*.

4. Answers may vary. McCall's placid palette of blues and violets and his lovely scenery—a dusk view of his gleaming city in a southwestern landscape of cactus, reddish mountains, a big sky of puffy clouds, and two more floating cities in the background—show that his voice is optimistic. Godwin's narrator's voice, which emphasizes the cruel math facing Barton in his decision about the stowaway, is grim and unrelenting. The contrast points to their respective views of technology: McCall's is positive and uplifting; Godwin's is negative and bleak.

EXTENSION AND ENRICHMENT

Writing Connections

1. Imagine what life would be like aboard Robert McCall's floating city. Use your imagination and details from the painting to write a short story about a boy or girl living in such a city. Concentrate on developing an interesting plot and on describing the setting. The short story will be evaluated on the basis of the following criteria:
   - The story concerns a boy or girl who lives in a futuristic floating city.
   - The plot of the story is interesting and contains a conflict and a resolution.
   - The setting is believably described.
   - The story is relatively free of errors in spelling, grammar, usage, and mechanics.

Crossing the Curriculum: Science and Technology

2. Watch a science fiction movie such as *2001: A Space Odyssey* or one of the *Star Trek* movies, and focus on the scientific advances presented in the movie. Then, write a brief review of these scientific advancements. Do you think they could ever come true? The review will be evaluated on the basis of the following criteria:
   - The review has a topic sentence stating the name of the movie and an overall opinion of its depiction of scientific advances.
   - The review includes details from the movie to support the reviewer's opinion of the scientific advances.
   - The review is relatively free of errors in spelling, grammar, usage, and mechanics.

BAKERY COUNTER
Wayne Thiebaud

Using Transparency 6

This transparency will complement the selection "Taste—The Final Frontier" by Esther Addley (Student Edition, Col. 3, p. 187). To complete the Looking at the Painting blackline master, students will have to read this newspaper article. Students should also be made aware of information in About the Art. This transparency may also be used with other selections.

Introducing the Painting

1. What kind of painting is this? What colors dominate the work, and what atmosphere do they create?

2. What is the focal point of the work? What effect does Thiebaud's composition have on the focal point?

3. Would you call this painting realistic? Explain your answer.

4. In view of the shapes and shadows in this work, why might Thiebaud have chosen these objects?

5. What might Thiebaud be saying about modern life? Do you think he wanted to be funny? Explain your answer.

Focusing on Background

About the Artist　The paint used by Wayne Thiebaud looks good enough to eat. In lush strokes and layering, he invests banal images—cake wedges, hot dogs, pie—with incongruous beauty and resonance.

Born in Mesa, Arizona, in 1920, Thiebaud began his long career by studying commercial art. At sixteen, he landed a job as an animation artist at the Disney studio, which led to freelance cartoon work. During World War II, he continued his cartoon efforts for an Army newspaper. After his discharge, he found work as a commercial illustrator. In 1949, Thiebaud enrolled at California State University in San José. A year later, at age thirty, and now sure he wanted to be a painter, he transferred to the Sacramento campus, where he received a B.A. and an M.A.

In 1958, on a leave of absence from teaching at Sacramento City College, he spent time in New York, where he met abstract expressionists Willem de Kooning and Franz Kline. Their forceful brush strokes influenced Thiebaud, but the lighter work of pop-based artist Jasper Johns caught his eye. Excited, he began small paintings based on images of displayed food, focusing on the basic shapes. Returning to California, he evolved the idea further by isolating the colorful triangles and circles of diner fare. In 1960, the San Francisco Museum of Art gave Thiebaud a solo show. Two years later, in New York, an exhibition launching pop art by Sidney Janis brought Thiebaud wide acclaim. He soon turned to figure painting, and during the 1970s and 1980s, he painted landscapes and San Francisco cityscapes. Displaying the formal interests of his early work, the land- and cityscapes found critical support.

About the Art　*Bakery Counter,* while vivid and evocative, also captures the artist's laconic visual wit. In this painting—funny, beautiful, and somewhat sad all at once—Thiebaud pushes the isolation of his still-life food to the extreme. Using the most basic shapes (rectangle, circle, squares) in the light of his formal pursuits in representation and composition, Thiebaud is able to depict very simply the absurdity of modern life.

As in most Thiebaud still lifes, the objects sit in a big, oily field of off-white. Layered with his warm brushwork, the space sets a stage that isolates his objects, which, he said, "are for me like characters in a play with costumes." But is *Bakery Counter* comedy or light drama? While funny, its loneliness recalls the work of Edward Hopper, whose mute urban scenes (including the iconic *Nighthawks,* with its late-night-diner customers behind a wall of glass) were a favorite of Thiebaud's.

Humanities Connection

History　The diner, that quintessential American locale, emerged in the 1930s, responding to the Depression and the quickening pace of modern life with cheap, fast fare. It spread from cities to suburbs and rural truck stops. In the forties, after World War II, diners became more prevalent. But it is the 1950s that most people associate with diners. Then, more than ever, hungry Americans wanted food fast and without fuss.

Collection 3 Narrator and Voice • Generating Research Questions   WORKSHEET **6**

BAKERY COUNTER
Wayne Thiebaud

Looking at the Painting

1. Some people see *Bakery Counter* as symbolic of the modern human condition. What feeling(s) might Thiebaud's painting symbolize? Cite aspects of the painting to support your answer.

_____

_____

_____

_____

2. How does Thiebaud's palette and content connect with the topic of Esther Addley's newspaper article "Taste—The Final Frontier"?

_____

_____

_____

_____

3. How does the mood of the painting compare with the mood of Addley's article?

_____

_____

_____

_____

4. Compare the tone of the painting with the tone of Addley's **voice** in "Taste—The Final Frontier." Refer to aspects of each work to support your comparison.

_____

_____

_____

_____

BAKERY COUNTER
Wayne Thiebaud

ANSWER KEY

Introducing the Painting

1. Answers may vary. This is a still life. Off-white and various pinks and browns dominate the work. The atmosphere is one of clean, cool emptiness.

2. Answers may vary. The focal point is the food in a display case. The composition is wide and very balanced. The case focuses viewers' attention on the food displayed.

3. Answers may vary. Most students will probably consider the painting fairly realistic, although some may see the painterly style and the expressive use of shadow and color as more subjective.

4. Answers may vary. Thiebaud was interested in these objects for the opportunity they provided to study and portray basic geometric shapes.

5. Answers may vary. Thiebaud may be commenting on the absurdity and isolation of modern life. Most students will see the intended humor in the work.

Looking at the Painting

1. Answers may vary. Thiebaud's painting may symbolize feelings of loneliness, isolation, and alienation.

2. Answers may vary. Thiebaud's off-white and cool colors are connected with the topic of spacecraft, which often are white. The food displayed unnaturally in a case is connected with the topic of food for astronauts by suggesting the environment of a spacecraft.

3. Answers may vary. Some students may think the mood of the painting is as light and comical as the mood of the newspaper article, whereas others may see the painting as sadder and more thoughtful than the article.

4. Answers may vary. All assessments of the tone of the painting are acceptable if they are supported by references to aspects of the work; the tone of Addley's voice in "Taste—The Final Frontier" is informal, witty, sassy, sarcastic, lighthearted, breezy, and so forth.

EXTENSION AND ENRICHMENT

Writing Connections

1. Consider this painting as a symbol of human loneliness, and write a screenplay scene that conveys that theme. Picture a diner that has Thiebaud's bakery case. Invent two characters that might be eating at this diner. Then, after describing the diner and characters to set your scene, create dialogue and actions that reinforce the theme of loneliness. The screenplay scene will be evaluated on the basis of the following criteria:
   - The screenplay scene is in an acceptable format and adequately describes the diner and the two characters.
   - The dialogue and action in the scene contribute to the theme of loneliness.
   - The scene is relatively free of errors in spelling, grammar, usage, and mechanics.

Crossing the Curriculum: Science

2. Wayne Thiebaud is famous for his pictures of food. But it is not likely that an astronaut would be able to take this kind of food along on a space trip. The fact that there is no gravity in space would mean that Thiebaud's beautiful pies and cakes would fly around the cabin! Research the kinds of foods astronauts bring into space. How are the foods prepared? How are they eaten? A good place to start your research would be on the internet site maintained by NASA.

Collection 4 Comparing Themes • Evaluating Arguments: Pro and Con

THE WALK
Marc Chagall

Using Transparency 7

Use this transparency with "It's Raining in Love" by Richard Brautigan (Student Edition, Col. 4, p. 251). To complete the Looking at the Painting blackline master, students will have to read this poem. Students should also be made aware of information in About the Art. This transparency may also be used with other selections.

Introducing the Painting

1. What is this couple doing? What clues suggest why they are outside of the town?

2. How would you describe the mood of the painting? How does Chagall create such a mood?

3. In what ways could this painting be considered fantastic or dreamlike? What is unusual about Chagall's use of color?

4. What might have been Chagall's reason for painting this scene and depicting the woman floating in the air?

5. In what way does Chagall stylize the land, the town, and the sky? What effect does this have on the work?

Focusing on Background

About the Artist Marc Chagall, one of the pivotal figures in twentieth-century art, lived a long, productive life that spanned several periods of turmoil in European history.

The artist was born Moshe Shagal (later changed to Marc Chagall, 1887–1985) to a poor couple in a small town in czarist Russia. Throughout his life, Chagall drew on memories of the Jewish community of his childhood for images in his art. In 1906, he began five years of art studies in St. Petersburg, Russia. But in 1910 he moved to Paris, where he was caught up in the city's artistic revolution and was influenced by the radical new works of Picasso and Matisse, as well as Sigmund Freud's ideas about dreams and the unconscious.

In 1914, Chagall and his family were trapped in Russia when World War I started. He worked in the country's Office of War Economy and was later appointed Commissar of Art for the town in which he was raised, Vitebsk. Chagall's nonpolitical art

was not appreciated by officials of the Soviet Union, so Chagall immigrated to France in 1922. He remained in France until conditions for Jews during World War II forced him to go into exile in the United States. He returned in 1948 to France, where he continued to create art with great energy. In addition to paintings, Chagall created murals, prints, mosaics, tapestries, sculptures, and stained-glass windows. He continued working almost until his death at the age of ninety-seven. Chagall's art is included in the collections of prestigious museums such as the State Russian Museum, the Guggenheim Museum, and the San Diego Museum of Art.

About the Art Love, the theme that permeates the imaginative, distinctive art of Marc Chagall, is highly evident in *The Walk* (or *The Promenade*). In the painting, Chagall's wife, Bella, floats through the air, pulled aloft by the power of the couple's love. Of course, the man who grasps Bella with one hand and holds a bird with the other is Chagall himself. Through this painting and many others, Chagall expressed his joy in his marriage to Bella. Chagall and Bella Rosenfeld, engaged for seven years, married in 1915. Chagall continued his series of artistic tributes to Bella even after her death in 1944.

In style as well as in theme, *The Walk* is typical of Chagall's paintings. Chagall created his own fantastic, dreamlike worlds on canvas filled with emotion, color, mystery, and magic. His use of color and sharp edges in this painting is reminiscent of much of his painting in the first half of the twentieth century. Two of the recurring symbols in Chagall's work are seen in *The Walk:* a couple, representing love, and floating figures, representing joy.

Humanities Connection

Psychology Sigmund Freud (1856–1939) created psychoanalysis, which he defined as the scientific study of the unconscious mind. His ideas about human emotions and motivations have had a profound effect on twentieth-century art and culture. Freud said that the unconscious mind influences conscious thought as well as actions and that unconscious memories of the past influence our attitudes and behaviors in the present.

NAME _____ CLASS _____ DATE _____

Collection 4 Comparing Themes • Evaluating Arguments:
Pro and Con

THE WALK
Marc Chagall

Looking at the Painting

1. What discovery or awakening might the two figures in this painting be celebrating?

_____

_____

_____

_____

2. In what sense could the title of Richard Brautigan's poem "It's Raining in Love" be appropriate for Chagall's painting?

_____

_____

_____

_____

3. Look again at the woman in *The Walk.* How does Chagall's idea contrast with lies 8 to 10 of Brautigan's poem?

_____

_____

_____

_____

4. Compare the **theme** of Brautigan's poem with the theme of Chagall's painting. Cite parts of each work to support your response.

_____

_____

_____

_____

The Walk

Collection 4 Comparing Themes • Evaluating Arguments: ANSWER KEY **7**
                Pro and Con

THE WALK
Marc Chagall

ANSWER KEY

Introducing the Painting

1. Answers may vary. The couple appears to be on a walk in green fields. A town lies in the distance behind them. A patterned red cloth on the ground, a decanter, and glass suggest that they are having a picnic.

2. Answers may vary. The mood could be described as happy, exuberant, or dreamlike. Such a mood is created by the cheerful expressions and actions of the couple and by the fanciful designs and colors around them.

3. Answers may vary. Dreamlike or fantastic elements include the floating woman; the bird in the man's hand; the stylized, sharp-edged designs; and the unusual green and black town and landscape.

4. Answers may vary. Chagall probably wanted to express the joy of a couple in love (actually Chagall and his wife, Bella). The woman may be floating because her spirits are high and she feels joyous and "light as air."

5. Answers may vary. Chagall uses quiltlike patches in the shape of diamonds, rectangles, and triangles to stylize the land, the town, and the sky. This pictorial approach unifies these elements of the scene, creating a sense of magical harmony.

Looking at the Painting

1. Answers may vary. The couple may be celebrating the discovery or awakening of their love and relationship, their joy in living, and the beauty around them.

2. Answers may vary. Brautigan's title could be appropriate for the painting in that Chagall shows an overcast sky that could break out in rain on his lovers; his woman figure could be seen as floating through the air like rain; and his depiction of the scene seems as if magic is emanating from the lovers and covers all the land like a blanket or rain.

3. Answers may vary. Chagall's idea shows how love is uplifting, as the woman is literally floating up off the ground, apparently lighter than air in

her surrender to love. In contrast, Brautigan uses line breaks and word position in lines 8 to 10 to show how "to examine, evaluate, compute" causes an opposite downward, or negative, movement in the speaker.

4. Answers may vary. The theme of Brautigan's poem is that unfolding love, or a crush, especially when its reciprocation is in doubt, is painful and difficult; lines such as "It makes me nervous" and "I get a little creepy" spell out this theme. Chagall's theme, on the other hand, seems to be that love has the magical power to lift us above our circumstances and to infuse the world with beauty; his floating woman and harmoniously lovely scene voice this theme.

EXTENSION AND ENRICHMENT

Writing Connections

1. Create lyrics for a song about the man and woman in Chagall's *The Walk*. The song should include references to the floating woman, the picnic, the bird in the man's hand, and the green town and landscape. Perform your song before the class. The song and performance will be evaluated on the basis of the following criteria:
   • The song's lyrics are based on images in Chagall's *The Walk*.
   • The lyrics reflect the general mood of the painting.

Crossing the Curriculum: Science

2. Chagall believed there was a harmony between love and nature. Take this idea outdoors to discover the natural world around you. Select one animal or plant and research it in books, in encyclopedias, on the Internet, or through other sources. Then, prepare an illustrated poster, perhaps using a bulletin board and colored paper, about your subject. The poster will be evaluated on the basis of the following criteria:
   • The poster reflects knowledge of the subject.
   • Significant facts are presented about the animal or plant.
   • The plant or animal is illustrated with drawings or pictures.
   • Elements are logically organized.

22

Collection 4   Comparing Themes • Evaluating Arguments: Pro and Con

TEACHING NOTES **8**

ARHATS BESTOWING ALMS UPON BEGGARS
Chou Chi-Ch'ang

Using Transparency 8

This transparency will complement the selection "The Parable of the Good Samaritan" from the King James Bible (Student Edition, Col. 4, p. 278). To complete the Looking at the Painting blackline master, students will have to read this Bible text. Students should also be made aware of information in About the Artist and the Art. This transparency may also be used with other selections.

Introducing the Painting

1. An arhat is a very holy Buddhist monk—in some ways like a Christian saint. How has Chou Chi-Ch'ang depicted the arhats and the beggars? Why might he have depicted the two groups so differently?

2. What does the artist's use of color in the painting add to the story or to the characters?

3. What do the arhats seem to be giving the beggars?

4. When you first looked at the painting, what were the first picture elements that drew your attention? Why?

5. Describe the differences in personal attitude, posture, and bearing between the arhats and the beggars.

Focusing on Background

About the Artist and the Art *Arhats Bestowing Alms upon Beggars* was painted in ink and natural pigments on silk by Chou Chi-Ch'ang in 1184. Arhats are holy Buddhist monks who have reached Nirvana, a state of detachment from worldly things and from the cycle of rebirth. They are shown standing on a cloud or heavenly firmament giving alms (charity—money, food, or clothes), in this case coins, to beggars. At the time this painting was done, the Song Dynasty in China provided an academy and scholarships to encourage the arts; the result was an especially fruitful artistic era for painting, ceramics, and bookprinting. The Song period (960–1279) thus continued the rich tradition of Chinese art begun during the Han Dynasty (202 B.C.–A.D. 220).

Several traditions in painting, as well as in stonework, ceramics, and calligraphy, had emerged in Chinese art by the time Chou Chi-Ch'ang painted at the imperial court. Popular subjects included realistic depictions of feasts and court activities, picturesque renderings of landscapes, detailed sketches of flowers and birds, and idealized portraits of religious figures. Chou Chi-Ch'ang incorporates several traditional elements, such as the bright colors of the arhats' robes; the serene expressions on their faces; the intricate, stylized tree; and the wispy, cloudlike designs that make up the surface on which the arhats stand.

Chou Chi-Ch'ang probably attended the imperial art academy founded by the emperor at the beginning of the Song Dynasty. The academy took promising students from all over the Chinese empire, had six grade levels, and offered courses in the painting of landscapes, birds and animals, flowers and bamboo, architecture, and both Buddhist and Taoist religious themes. The apprentices and artists from the academy lived at the imperial court and created the many splendid artifacts—both useful and decorative—that filled the opulent household of the emperor and his courtiers.

The Song emperors not only financed the imperial art academy, but some of them also became accomplished painters and calligraphers in their own right. In the twelfth century, for example, the emperor Hui Tsang sent examples of his own work to the art academy once a month so that the students could follow in his artistic footsteps.

Humanities Connection

History The Song Dynasty ended when the Mongol warrior Kublai Khan, who had taken over much of China, finally succeeded in conquering the Song emperor. Kublai Khan abolished the Song imperial art academy. As a result, the greatest painters of Kublai Khan's Yuan Dynasty (1260–1368) turned to scholars and literature for their inspiration, not to the imperial court.

Collection 4 Comparing Themes • Evaluating Arguments: WORKSHEET 8
                Pro and Con

ARHATS BESTOWING ALMS UPON BEGGARS
Chou Chi-Ch'ang

Looking at the Painting

1. What in the painting reminds you of fables or tales that you have heard about or read?

_____

_____

_____

_____

2. Consider the beggars in the painting and the wounded man in "The Parable of the Good Samaritan." How might their attitudes toward their benefactors differ?

_____

_____

_____

_____

3. How might the good Samaritan show a detachment from worldly things as the arhats traditionally do?

_____

_____

_____

_____

4. In what ways is the behavior of the arhats in the painting similar to and/or different from that of the good Samaritan? Is the **theme** of each work the same?

_____

_____

_____

_____

Collection 4   Comparing Themes • Evaluating Arguments: ANSWER KEY **8**
             Pro and Con

ARHATS BESTOWING ALMS UPON BEGGARS
Chou Chi-Ch'ang

ANSWER KEY

Introducing the Painting

1. Chou depicts the arhats as divine beings who look well fed and serene. The beggars, on the other hand, are sketched to look barely human. The artist might have done this to show the great contrast between the physical and spiritual situations of the two groups.

2. Answers may vary. The color makes the arhats seem richer and more important than the colorless beggars.

3. The arhat in the front seems to be dropping coins to the beggars. The other arhats may be planning to offer the beggars something, too.

4. Answers may vary. Students may say that they first looked at the arhat in the front because of his red, white, and blue robes; they then looked at the dark arhat because of his red robe; and, finally, they looked at the disheveled beggars groveling at the bottom of the frame.

5. Answers may vary. The arhats look detached, serene, and poised, whereas the beggars look hopeless, ugly, and perhaps a little frightening.

Looking at the Painting

1. Answers may vary. Students may mention the fact that the arhats are floating on a magic cloud and that the beggars are, in effect, finding much-needed money falling from the sky, the sort of thing that happens in genie or leprechaun stories or in "The Goose That Laid the Golden Egg."

2. Answers may vary. The beggars have various expressions; some look grateful, some do not. We don't know what the wounded man felt, but he probably felt grateful to the Samaritan for saving his life.

3. Answers may vary. The good Samaritan shows a detachment from money when he gives the innkeeper money for the injured man's care and says he will repay him for additional expenses.

4. Answers may vary. The arhats and the good Samaritan both help those in need, but the arhats are more detached from the beggars and are not seen nursing or caring for them as the Samaritan does for the wounded man. The theme of each work is essentially the same: that it is kind, just, and loving to help those in need and that this generosity and rising above material concerns emulates God.

EXTENSION AND ENRICHMENT

Writing Connections

1. Write a dialogue between the arhats and the beggars, characterizing the different individuals. What does it feel like to be a holy person giving to the poor, and how might the beggars feel about the arhats' charity? You might include details that explain how the arhats came upon the beggars and why the beggars are so poor. Your dialogue will be evaluated on the basis of the following criteria:
   • The dialogue depicts the characters, situations, and feelings of some of the arhats and beggars.
   • The dialogue is relatively free of errors in spelling, grammar, usage, and mechanics.

Crossing the Curriculum: Social Studies

2. Using encyclopedias, newspapers, the Internet, and other sources, research the topic of world hunger, and then prepare a poster and a short report for the class. Organize your poster and your report around different regions or countries. Find out what is considered enough daily food per person by international organizations such as the United Nations. Then, create a chart for the poster comparing the regions or countries you chose. Include in the chart data such as money spent on food per day, the amount of food available to the local population, or the number of relief organizations helping a certain area. Your poster and report will be evaluated on the basis of the following criteria:
   • The poster and report compare several aspects of world hunger in different regions or countries.
   • The chart is easy to read and the accompanying text is relatively free of errors in spelling, grammar, usage, and mechanics.

THE KITCHEN WINDOW
Leo Whelan

Using Transparency 9

This transparency will complement the selection "Lamb to the Slaughter" by Roald Dahl (Student Edition, Col. 5, p. 316). To complete the Looking at the Painting blackline master, students will have to read this short story. Students should also be made aware of information in About the Art. This transparency may also be used with other selections.

Introducing the Painting

1. What is the woman in the painting doing? How would you describe her expression?

2. Would you identify the scene in the painting as realistic or fanciful? Explain your answer.

3. What effects of light does Whelan emphasize in this painting?

4. What does the title of the painting suggest about the artist's purpose?

5. Does this interior scene appeal to you? Why or why not?

Focusing on Background

About the Artist Leo Whelan (1892–1956) was a prominent portrait painter in Dublin during the first half of the twentieth century. A native of Dublin, Whelan attended Belvedere College. His exceptional talents were noted early by the distinguished portraitist Sir William Orpen, with whom Whelan studied at the Dublin Metropolitan School of Art. Whelan had several important boosts at the beginning of his art career. In 1911, he first showed a painting at the Royal Hibernian Academy; during his lifetime, he exhibited 263 more paintings there. In 1916, he received a scholarship from the Royal Dublin Society for his painting *The Doctor's Visit,* which now hangs in the National Gallery of Ireland.

Whelan's renown, as well as the number of his awards, grew during the 1920s. He was among the Irish artists who exhibited at the *Exposition d'Art Irlandais* in Paris in 1922. The Royal Hibernian Academy made him a member in 1924. That same year, his portrait *The Gipsy* was exhibited at the Academy, securing his fame as an artist. Whelan received a medal in 1926 at the Tailteann Games for his portrait of the vice-provost of Dublin's Trinity College.

About the Art In addition to many portraits, Leo Whelan painted some interior scenes that have been highly praised, including *The Kitchen Window.* He painted several realistic interiors of kitchens, each showing a person preparing food, surrounded by vegetables and cooking utensils. The woman standing at the kitchen table in this painting is probably Whelan's sister Frances, whom he painted in other interior settings. The room depicted is most likely the basement of the artist's Dublin house. In his portraits, Whelan usually distributed the light evenly, but in this interior study, he concentrated on the dramatic effects of light and shade (chiaroscuro), creating a scene that could be called theatrical. This interior is representative of both Whelan's technical skill and his portraiture style.

Among painters whom Whelan admired were John Singer Sargent, the American portrait painter; the Spanish artist Velázquez; and seventeenth-century Dutch painters, such as Jan Vermeer, who often portrayed people pursuing leisure activities in small rooms with window lighting. In style and composition, *The Kitchen Window* is reminiscent of Vermeer's oil painting *Girl Reading a Letter at an Open Window,* 1657.

Humanities Connection

Social Studies Dubliners live in a historic atmosphere, enjoying architecture dating back from medieval time. Their city, near Dublin Bay, is the largest city in the Republic of Ireland and the country's capital. It is also the island's cultural, industrial, and commercial center. The city's wide streets, many squares, and low buildings date from the late eighteenth century. Dubliners experience cool summers and mild winters, and are accustomed to about thirty inches of rain per year.

NAME _____ CLASS _____ DATE _____

ELEMENTS OF LITERATURE   **FOURTH COURSE**   **FINE ART**

Collection 5 Irony and Ambiguity • Generating Research Questions and Evaluating Sources

WORKSHEET 9

THE KITCHEN WINDOW
Leo Whelan

Looking at the Painting

1. List three aspects of Whelan's painting that capture your imagination.

_____

_____

_____

_____

2. How do the setting, lighting, and figure in Whelan's painting evoke the **mood** of Roald Dahl's story "Lamb to the Slaughter"?

_____

_____

_____

_____

3. The emotion of the moment Whelan captures is **ambiguous.** What moment in Dahl's story could it portray?

_____

_____

_____

_____

4. In Dahl's story, the murder weapon itself, a "harmless" leg of lamb, is **ironic.** Given the scene in the painting, how might Whelan's lighting be seen as ironic?

_____

_____

_____

The Kitchen Window

27

Collection 5 Irony and Ambiguity • Generating Research Questions and Evaluating Sources

THE KITCHEN WINDOW
Leo Whelan

ANSWER KEY

Introducing the Painting

1. Answers may vary. It appears that she is polishing a piece of silver. Her expression may be described as calm, serious, tolerant, or perhaps slightly surprised.

2. Answers may vary. The scene is generally painted realistically—especially the depiction of the woman, including her figure and dress; the peeling paint on the cupboards, and the red-and-white check-patterned cloth; the silver objects; the window panes; and the lighting.

3. Answers may vary. He emphasizes the effects of strong natural light on the interior of a dim room, the light's direction, and the shadows and reflections caused by the light.

4. Answers may vary. The title suggests that Whelan was more interested in showing the window, specifically the light coming through the window, than he was in depicting the woman. He may have been more interested in the dramatic effects of light on the interior than in the interior itself.

5. Answers may vary. Some students may like the lighting effects and the darkness and heaviness of the room, while others may prefer a lighter, brighter, more modern kitchen.

Looking at the Painting

1. Answers may vary. Possible responses are the view outside the window, the woman's identity and history, and the condition of the cupboard.

2. Answers may vary. The apparently homey setting, the shadowy and mysterious lighting, and the emotionally opaque figure all can evoke the dark, suspenseful mood of Dahl's story.

3. Answers may vary. Though the action of the woman figure in *The Kitchen Window* doesn't exactly match the actions described in the story, the painting could portray the moment after Mary puts the leg of lamb in the oven or the moment when the police first arrive at her house.

4. Answers may vary. Since the scene in the painting shows an everyday kitchen in which an ordinary woman is involved in the simple domestic chore of polishing silver, Whelan's lighting—which is shadowy and highly dramatic—can be seen as ironic because it confers drama and mystery on an apparently ordinary situation.

EXTENSION AND ENRICHMENT

Literary Connections

1. Imagine that the woman in the painting is a character in a one-person play. In the play, the woman tells about her life, dreams, and imaginings. While she is working, she may even talk to objects in the room or to the window. Write a scene from this one-person play based on the images in *The Kitchen Window*. The scene will be evaluated on the basis of the following criteria:
   • The woman's character in *The Kitchen Window* is developed during the scene through her own words and thoughts.
   • Standard form is followed for writing descriptions and dialogue in a play.
   • The scene is relatively free of errors in spelling, grammar, usage, and mechanics.

Crossing the Curriculum: Interior Design

2. Use your imagination and experiences to design your dream kitchen. How big would the kitchen be? What would the floor plan look like? What would you have in the kitchen? Design a kitchen that would be ideal for you (the kitchen may be in an apartment or a house, and may be large or small). Describe the details of your kitchen in writing, and draw a floor plan that includes labels identifying major appliances, windows, doors, and furniture. The kitchen design will be evaluated on the basis of the following criteria:
   • Thought and imagination are evident in the design.
   • The floor plan is clearly drawn and labeled.
   • The description is relatively free of errors in spelling, grammar, usage, and mechanics.

RAPID TRANSIT
Doug Webb

Using Transparency 10

This transparency will complement the selection "Notes from a Bottle" by James Stevenson (Student Edition, Col. 5, p.374), To complete the Looking at the Painting blackline master, students will have to read this short story. Students should also be made aware of information in About the Art. This transparency may also be used with other selections.

Introducing the Painting

1. What city is depicted in Webb's painting, and what is unusual about the scene?

2. What style or school of art would describe *Rapid Transit*? Why?

3. In what sense is Webb's painting realistic?

4. Explain the irony of the painting in relation to its title.

5. Do you think Webb intended his painting to be humorous or serious? Explain your answer.

Focusing on Background

About the Artist Webb was born in 1946 in Istanbul, Turkey, where his father, a U.S. Army intelligence officer, was stationed. The family soon moved back to the United States, and he grew up mostly in California. Always drawn to the arts, Webb studied acting in high school and college. After college he worked as a professional musician, playing the bass. Fine art, however, had always been his first career choice. Largely self-taught, Webb began painting seriously in the late 1970s, using watercolor and mostly producing realistic portraits. But even in early realist landscapes, the artist experimented with the juxtaposition of reality and illusion. His work slowly grew stranger.

In 1981, Webb landed his first solo show at the Yves Arman Gallery in New York City. With his style by this time planted in the surrealist tradition of René Magritte (1898–1967), Webb attracted public and critical attention. By the mid-1980s he was working completely in acrylics, and his playfulness had fully emerged. Paintings such as *Stress Management,* a giant bouquet of flowers atop Manhattan's Madison Square Garden, and *Critical Mass,* four colorful marbles holding their own

against the pyramids of Giza, Egypt, display signature Webb elements. Composite images and shifts in scale between the monumental and the mundane charge the artist's work with a tongue-in-cheek tension.

About the Art *Rapid Transit* showcases Webb's specific surrealist stance. But his work has a deadpan feel all its own. This photorealist midtown-Manhattan corner relaxes the eye by offering a familiar setting rendered without flourish. Lulling viewers into a prosaic urban landscape in this way, Webb juxtaposes a jarring whitewater river that barrels down the street. A quintet of rafters seems unaware, or nonplussed, that they are floating down Fifty-seventh Street. And the few pedestrians either cannot see this river or do not care.

Webb pairs very real things in a very unreal way. The ironically titled *Rapid Transit,* like much of his art, can suggest the computer-generated images of movie special effects. Webb, however, slowly crafts his work. First, he sketches an imagined image. Then, he photographs the scenes or objects that he needs. Sometimes he builds a scale model of his picture, usually in clay. Finally, Webb begins to paint the canvas, working in layers that he coats with transparent glaze to add texture and depth. A painting of his may take as long as six months to complete. In the end, Webb has a work of technical artistry, playfully ironic and, ultimately, ambiguous.

Humanities Connection

Art History Surrealism, an artistic and literary movement, was founded in 1924 by the French poet and art critic André Breton (1896–1966). Breton wanted to find the point where the real and the imaginary are no longer perceived as contradictory. Like Breton's poems, the films of Luis Buñuel (1900–1983), and the paintings of Giorgio De Chirico (1888–1978), along with those of Magritte and Dali, used irrational combinations of images. Surrealism, following in the footsteps of Freud, looked to dreams and the unconscious mind and, in so doing, formed an aesthetic pillar of twentieth-century modernism.

Collection 5   Irony and Ambiguity • Generating Research Questions and Evaluating Sources

RAPID TRANSIT
Doug Webb

Looking at the Painting

1. In view of the scene in Webb's painting, how is the reaction of the pedestrians and the motorists **ironic**?

_____

_____

_____

_____

2. How does the depiction of water in Webb's painting differ from that in James Stevenson's short story "Notes from a Bottle"?

_____

_____

_____

_____

3. Compare the **tone** of Stevenson's story with the tone of Webb's painting. Which is more **ambiguous**? Cite aspects of each work to support your answers.

_____

_____

_____

_____

4. Explain how Webb's painting and Stevenson's story both use **irony** to comment on society. Why might New York City serve as the setting in both works?

_____

_____

_____

_____

RAPID TRANSIT
Doug Webb

ANSWER KEY

Introducing the Painting

1. Answers may vary. The painting depicts New York City. The most unusual aspect of the scene is the rafters paddling on a river rushing through the city streets, but the lack of reaction from the passersby is also unusual.

2. Surrealism is the style or school of art that describes *Rapid Transit*. The use of realism to represent fantastic scenes and objects and the juxtaposition of incongruous or dreamlike images are elements of this style.

3. Answers may vary. Webb's painting is realistic in its representation of the city streets and buildings to the human figures and the water, all rendered with photorealist objectivity.

4. Answers may vary. The title of the painting, *Rapid Transit*, refers to the rafters navigating rapids down New York's streets; the term *rapid transit* also refers, ironically, to subways, a major part of real life in New York City.

5. Answers may vary. Most students will probably think that Webb intended his painting to be humorous. Some, however, may see a more serious implication: a city so hardened and hurried that the sudden magic of a rushing river in its midst does not even raise an eyebrow.

Looking at the Painting

1. Answers may vary. With a rural whitewater river rushing right down the city streets, one would expect pedestrians and motorists to be amazed or concerned, but, ironically, they seem to just go about their business.

2. Answers may vary. The depiction of water in Webb's painting suggests a rural rather than an urban setting and does not seem threatening, whereas the water in Stevenson's story, dirty and carrying an occasional body, threatens the characters and is likely to cover the city.

3. Answers may vary. The tone of Stevenson's story is bleak as the narrator relates the grim parties of the doomed urbanites. The tone of

Webb's painting seems lighter and more sarcastic and can also be seen as funny or biting.

4. Answers may vary. Webb's painting uses irony to comment on the human "rat race," and Stevenson uses irony to show people's hardness and disillusionment. New York may be the setting in both works because these qualities, insensitive bustle and sad disillusionment seem prevalent in the popular conception of the city.

EXTENSION AND ENRICHMENT

Writing Connections

1. How would you react if a river came rushing through your town? Write a short story that centers on such an event. Use vivid description to portray the deluge, referring to actual locations in your town. Show the reactions of at least two characters, and try to incorporate at least one instance of irony. Your story can use any tone: suspenseful, funny, or sad. The short story will be evaluated on the basis of the following criteria:
   • The short story uses actual locations, shows at least two characters' reactions, and has at least one use of irony.
   • The story has a beginning, a middle, and an end.
   • The story is relatively free of errors in spelling, grammar, usage, and mechanics.

Crossing the Curriculum:
Art / Art History

2. Do an illustrated research paper on surrealism. Use the library or the Internet to find out who started this school of art and where. Include the most notable painters of the school, and explain their style and influences. Then, pick a favorite surrealist painting, and use colored pencils or pastels to copy it. Give a brief analysis of the painting. The illustrated paper will be evaluated on the basis of the following criteria:
   • The paper includes information on the origins and most notable surrealist painters.
   • The paper includes a copy of a surrealist work.
   • The paper is relatively free of errors in spelling, grammar, usage, and mechanics.

THE OLD MAN AND DEATH
Joseph Wright of Derby

Using Transparency 11

This transparency will complement the selection "The Masque of the Red Death" by Edgar Allan Poe (Student Edition, Col. 6, p. 418). To complete the Looking at the Painting blackline master, students will have to read this short story. Students should also be made aware of information in About the Art. This transparency may also be used with other selections.

Introducing the Painting

1. Describe the palette and lighting in the painting. How do these elements affect the mood of the work?

2. Why might Wright have set his scene in a natural landscape? What aspects create an air of Gothic horror?

3. How does the artist express the old man's fear?

4. How does Wright depict the relationship between the architecture and nature? What might this relationship symbolize?

5. What idea do you think the artist intended to express about people's imaginations and emotions?

Focusing on Background

About the Artist Joseph Wright of Derby (1734–1797) is considered an eighteenth-century original.

Born in the Midland region of Derby, England, Wright grew up in a center of the nascent Industrial Revolution. His childhood interest in science and technology stemmed from this exposure to the new inventions that were defining the era. By the age of sixteen, Wright had also developed a fascination with art. Showing impressive skill, he began formal art training in London around the time of his seventeenth birthday, in the studio of Thomas Hudson (1701–1779).

In the 1760s, Wright began a series of "Candle Light" paintings, in which he explored the effects of flame-light sources and shadows on various scientific subjects. This work was shown in London in 1765 in Wright's first exhibition at the Society of Artists. In the 1780s, Wright worked mostly on landscapes, many of Italian subjects, such as Mount

Vesuvius and the Colosseum. During the decade his asthma grew worse, and he became more high-strung. He continued to paint in a more Romantic style, however, up to his death in his hometown of Derby.

About the Art In *The Old Man and Death,* Wright depicts one of Aesop's fables in a Gothic style. The story concerns an old man, tired of coping with life's hardships, who drops his load of sticks and calls upon Death to take him away from his burdens. When he is face to face with the Grim Reaper, however, the old man changes his mind and persuades Death to go away. At the end of the fable, the man, as happens after a brush with death, sees life from a new perspective. Wright's painting captures the most terrifying moment of the story. The image of Death—a beckoning skeleton, arrow in hand—the old man's terror, and the overgrown ruins fill the work with Gothic atmosphere.

The anatomically correct skeleton shows Wright's attention to the scientific study of nature, and his fondness for the ideal beauty of natural landscapes comes through in the picturesque river setting. At the same time, his preoccupation with light can be read in the sharp contrasts on every twig. Wright knew how to render storms and night scenes, but he paints a beautiful day here, as if to show that life is worth living. Still, things do change for the worse. The gnarly dead tree limb at the center and the decay of the building palpably speak of death. They also remind us, with great Gothic flair, that the crumbly and the creepy can be gorgeous.

Humanities Connection

Art History It took centuries for artists to accurately portray the human figure, let alone its skeleton. The great leap took place in the 1400s, during the Renaissance. Not satisfied with their knowledge of the human form, artists such as Leonardo da Vinci became curious about the structure of the body and engaged in clandestine dissections of cadavers. The sketchbooks of da Vinci record his influential anatomical drawings. Michelangelo's muscled figures are convincing because they are based on a knowledge of anatomy.

Collection 6 Symbolism and Allegory • Synthesizing Sources   WORKSHEET **11**

THE OLD MAN AND DEATH
Joseph Wright of Derby

Looking at the Painting

1. Do you think Wright intended the viewer to view Death as a real creature? Could his painting, which is based on a fable by Aesop, be considered an **allegory**?

_____

_____

_____

_____

2. In what ways does Wright's depiction of Death relate to Edgar Allan Poe's specter in his short story "The Masque of the Red Death"?

_____

_____

_____

_____

3. Compare the setting of Wright's Gothic painting with that of Poe's horror story.

_____

_____

_____

_____

4. How do both Wright and Poe use **symbolism** to create atmosphere and express a dark truth? Which artist do you think uses symbols for better effect?

_____

_____

_____

_____

THE OLD MAN AND DEATH
Joseph Wright of Derby

ANSWER KEY

Introducing the Painting

1. Answers may vary. The palette—earthy brown, light blue, and green—is fairly upbeat, while the light has the contrast and deep shadows of early morning or late afternoon on a sunny day. The bright sky and upper area of the ruins convey a positive mood, but the foreground, where Death looms, is darker and adds a gloomy feel.

2. Answers may vary. Wright may have been emphasizing that a meeting with Death can occur anywhere, even amid natural beauty, or he may have thought that the isolated setting would add to the horror of the encounter.

3. Answers may vary. The artist depicts the man with his mouth slightly agape, his eyes bulging, his hand up in defense, and his body tensed and recoiling.

4. Answers may vary. Wright depicts the building in a state of crumbling ruin and surrounded by natural vegetation, which is actually growing on the structure. This depiction might symbolize that everything decays and that nature eventually reclaims humans and what is human-made.

5. Answers may vary. The artist may have intended to express the idea that people's imaginations and emotions can create frightening images and ideas that often cause great pain and unnecessary distress.

Looking at the Painting

1. Answers may vary. Wright intended to create a scary picture of Death that could strike some viewers as real and others as purely symbolic. The work could be considered an allegory of aging and the fear of dying.

2. Answers may vary. Wright's depiction of Death, like Poe's in "The Masque of the Red Death," is based on a human figure, is meant to be frightening, and is both literal and symbolic.

3. Answers may vary. The setting of Wright's painting is old ruins on a beautiful stretch of land along a river or lake, whereas Poe's setting

is a Gothic castle with rooms decorated in a fantastic, but somewhat morbid, color scheme.

4. Answers may vary. Wright uses a skeleton to symbolize death, and his dead tree limbs and crumbling ruins create a gloomy atmosphere of decay; Poe uses a grotesque figure to symbolize the plague and death, and the variation of his colored rooms, from blue to red-and-black, adds symbolic weight and a somewhat morbid atmosphere. Opinions of which symbolism is more effective will vary.

EXTENSION AND ENRICHMENT

Writing Connections

1. Write a short story in the Gothic horror tradition. Try to create a sense of terror and gloom in your spooky tale, and use an appropriately creepy setting, like a haunted castle. See if you can generate suspense, and be sure to include sensory details that will sustain the overall atmosphere of gloom and dread. The short story will be evaluated on the basis of the following criteria:
   • The short story uses a Gothic setting and attempts to generate suspense.
   • The story uses sensory details to create a scary mood.
   • The story is relatively free of errors in spelling, grammar, usage, and mechanics.

Crossing the Curriculum: Drama

2. The subject of Wright's painting comes from a fable of Aesop. In the school or public library, find the story in a book of fables. After studying the story, adapt it for the screen as a short horror movie. (Use the library or the Internet to find an example of accepted screenplay format.) Remember that you can change or add details to create suspense or horror. The screenplay will be evaluated on the basis of the following criteria:
   • The screenplay is clearly based on Aesop's fable of "The Old Man and Death."
   • The work is in an acceptable screenplay format.
   • The screenplay is relatively free of errors in spelling, grammar, usage, and mechanics.

TEACHING NOTES **12**

STUDY OF CLOUDS AT HAMPSTEAD
John Constable

Using Transparency 12

This transparency will complement the selection "A Storm in the Mountains" by Aleksandr Solzhenitsyn (Student Edition, Col. 7, p. 458). To complete the Looking at the Painting blackline master, students will have to read this prose poem. Students should also be made aware of information in About the Art. This transparency may also be used with other selections.

Introducing the Painting

1. What kind of painting is this? What are the dominant colors in the work?

2. Do you consider this painting realistic? Explain your answer.

3. Do you think Constable painted this picture slowly or quickly? Does his style of applying paint have any effect on the picture?

4. This painting is less than twelve inches wide. Do you think Constable captures the great expanse of his subject in this small area? Why or why not?

5. What do you think Constable intended to convey in this picture?

Focusing on Background

About the Artist The painter Henry Fuseli, a contemporary of John Constable (1776–1837), noted that Constable landscapes are "picturesque, and of a fine color; but he makes me call for my great coat and umbrella." Constable made epic efforts to capture up-to-the-minute conditions in the English countryside, and in his pictures the clouds often seem to roil, threatening to storm.

Constable also saw cloudy periods in his art career. Though he showed early talent, his originality evolved slowly. He decided to be an artist at the age of twenty-three, joining the Royal Academy School. After spending years working in the manner of Thomas Gainsborough (1727–1788), Constable developed his own approach, striving to depict scenery more realistically. Just as William Wordsworth (1770–1850) discarded the "poetic diction" of the time, Constable rejected pictorial traditions of fellow landscape painters, who, he said, "were always running after pictures, seeking the truth at second hand." Instead, he looked to seventeenth-century

Dutch landscapists, mainly Jacob van Ruisdael (1628–1682), whose moody work would be a major influence.

During the 1820s, Constable slowly gained recognition, with *The Hay Wain* (1821) winning a gold medal at the Paris Salon of 1824. While he never gained wide acclaim in England, he was popular in France, where he influenced key artists, including Eugene Delacroix (1798–1863), the great Romanticist. In his art, Constable sought to render the effects of changing light in the open air on the movement of clouds across the sky. To portray these changes, he abandoned fine finish, opting to portray sunlight in daubs of pure white or bright yellow and to capture storms with rough, fast brushwork. His love of the countryside in Suffolk and Hampstead, where he resided from 1821 to his death, is palpable in his work.

About the Art "No two days are alike, nor even two hours," John Constable remarked about capturing the changing skies over Suffolk and Hampstead. *Study of Clouds at Hampstead* shows Constable's feel for nature studies. "Good painting," he told his friend John Dunthorne, "can only be obtained by contemplation and incessant labor. . . . I shall make laborious studies from nature—and endeavor to get an unaffected representation of the scenes that employ me." In this study, with its brewing clouds, he boldly mixes color right on the surface. Raw white fades to cerulean blue and watery gray in poetic transition. On the cliff, at the lower right, Constable captures shade with impressionistic blobs of deep green and black.

Humanities Connection

Art History Landscape painting was not always an effort to depict things as they appear. In Chinese art, for example, landscapes display a long tradition of stylized formality, with nature bent to symbolize themes. Pre-Renaissance Western art relegated nature to the background, where it flatly sat without the illusion of three-dimensional perspective. While they added the appearance of depth, Renaissance painters left nature in the background of portraits and religious pictures. It was only in the 1600s that Dutch artists began to paint the realistic natural landscape as a subject in itself.

Collection 7 Poetry

STUDY OF CLOUDS AT HAMPSTEAD
John Constable

Looking at the Painting

1. Constable's *Study of Clouds at Hampstead* has been called "poetic." Do you think it conveys an emotion or an idea in a way that poetry can? Explain your answer.

_____

_____

_____

_____

2. Compare Constable's palette with the colors Aleksandr Solzhenitsyn describes in his prose poem "A Storm in the Mountains." Then, compare the mood of each work.

_____

_____

_____

_____

3. How might Constable's painting and Solzhenitsyn's prose poem be related in their view of nature?

_____

_____

_____

_____

4. Do you think Constable's painting communicates the wonder of nature as well as Solzhenitsyn's prose poem? Cite imagery from each work to support your answer.

_____

_____

_____

_____

36

STUDY OF CLOUDS AT HAMPSTEAD
John Constable

- -

ANSWER KEY

Introducing the Painting

1. This is a landscape painting. Varying whites, grays, and blues dominate the work.

2. Answers may vary. Many students will see the naturalistic representation of sky and land as realistic, while others may feel that the blurry paint effects and expressive brush strokes are unrealistic.

3. Answers may vary. Most students will think that Constable painted this picture quickly because of the nature of the brush strokes and the loose depiction of lines. Students may see that the expressive application of paint gives the picture a sense of immediacy and emotion.

4. Answers may vary. While there is general agreement that Constable was masterful in conveying great expanse in small-scale work, some students may feel that his painterly brush strokes and traditional realism fail to convey the grand size of his scene.

5. Answers may vary. Constable intended to convey the formation of clouds in the sky, the quality of light, and the effect of that light on a part of the land at Hampstead on the day that he painted the picture.

Looking at the Painting

1. Answers may vary. Some students may note that Constable's painting aptly portrays the grandeur and awesome beauty of nature, qualities that have long sparked human emotions and the ideas expressed in poetry. Others may think that the painting is too literal in its realism to be poetic.

2. In addition to white, gray, and blue, Constable uses green and black for the trees and tinges his sky with yellow, pink, violet, and mauve; Solzhenitsyn describes the black of the night storm and the white, pink, and violet of lightning. Most students will see the mood of Constable's painting as lighter and less dramatic than that of Solzhenitsyn's prose poem.

3. Answers may vary. Constable's painting and Solzhenitsyn's prose poem both seem to view nature as an awesome, wondrous phenomenon subject to dramatic change and staggering beauty.

4. Answers may vary. Some students will find that the drama and human perspective of Solzhenitsyn's prose poem better communicate the wonder of nature, whereas others may find that Constable's landscape, a naturalistic picture, better captures that wonder in letting nature speak for itself.

EXTENSION AND ENRICHMENT

Writing Connections

1. Write a poem that captures the wonder of clouds. Observe the sky on a day when clouds are on display. Take notes on the shapes and colors, and record the wind direction, time of day, and quality of light. Then convert your observations to poetry, using rhythm, sensory images, and figurative language to express the wonder of the sky. Title your poem "Study of Clouds at . . ." The poem will be evaluated on the basis of the following criteria:
   - The poem describes the clouds in the sky and the quality of the light on a given day.
   - The poem attempts to create a rhythm and has at least one sensory image and one figurative description.
   - The poem is relatively free of errors in spelling, grammar, usage, and mechanics.

Crossing the Curriculum: Science

2. What's the difference between cumulus and cirrus clouds? Use an encyclopedia, the library, and/or the Internet to research the nature of clouds. Then, write a two-page paper on these beautiful natural phenomena. Be sure to include scientific information on the formation, composition, and classification of the various types of clouds. The research paper will be evaluated on the basis of the following criteria:
   - The research paper presents accurate information about clouds, written in the student's own words.
   - The paper includes information on the formation, composition, and classification of the various cloud types.
   - The paper is relatively free of errors in spelling, grammar, usage, and mechanics.

SUMMER
Winslow Homer

Using Transparency 13

Use this transparency with "Shall I Compare Thee to a Summer's Day?" by William Shakespeare (Student Edition, Col. 7, p. 493). To complete the Looking at the Painting blackline master, students will have to read this sonnet. Students should also be made aware of information in About the Art. This transparency may also be used with other selections.

Introducing the Painting

1. What is the woman in the painting doing?

2. What is the focal point of the painting? What draws our attention to this focal point?

3. What creates balance in the painting?

4. What mood do you think the artist was trying to convey in this painting?

5. What do you think the artist's attitude is toward the woman figure in the painting?

Focusing on Background

About the Artist Although Winslow Homer (1836–1910) traveled extensively, he is most closely identified with New England, where he was born. When he was six, his family moved from Boston to Cambridge, Massachusetts, and it was there that he began to develop his love for and fascination with nature. Homer began his career working as an apprentice to a local lithographer, but on his twenty-first birthday, after completing his apprenticeship, he left lithography to embark upon a career as a freelance illustrator.

After achieving considerable success with his illustrating, Homer left Boston for New York in 1859, as New York had become the nation's art and publishing center. In New York, Homer free-lanced for the magazine *Harper's Weekly*. When the Civil War broke out, the magazine sent him on several trips to the front to draw the daily life of the troops. Soon afterward, Homer made his first oil paintings. Ten years later, he began to paint seriously with watercolors. In 1883, Homer established a residence and studio in Prout's Neck, Maine,

where he spent the remaining twenty-seven years of his life. The oil paintings he produced while living in Prout's Neck rank among his greatest works.

About the Art Winslow Homer often painted women engaged in active pastimes and faithfully reproduced all of the details of their attire—showing with honesty and humor the wind-whipped flounced skirts, bedraggled bathing costumes, and elegant, hoop-skirted young girls ice skating in Central Park. Although Homer did not idealize women in his paintings to the extent that many of his colleagues did, his female figures often appear as decorative creatures and stylized types, rather than as individuals.

Homer first became seriously interested in watercolors in 1873, the year before he painted *Summer*. Watercolor paintings were easy to produce quickly. They were also easy for Homer to sell, so he was able to stop his illustration work and devote his time entirely to painting. In this work, the artist used gouache, rich water-based pigments that produce deep color and a flat finish. The medium is common in illustration, and Homer uses it to render muted, rich color that is soft and pleasing to the eye. *Summer* is typical of much of the artist's early work in that it depicts American country life without sentimentality. It also presents a scene of elegance and comfortable living and, like most of Homer's work, focuses on the pleasant aspects of lives pleasantly lived.

Humanities Connection

Social Studies Since Homer's day, fashions for women have become much less elaborate. During the 1800s, most women usually had to wear long-sleeved, full-length dresses with petticoats underneath, even in the summertime. Since 1900, women's clothing has gradually become more simplified. By the 1920s, women did not have to keep their arms and legs covered in hot weather. After World War II (1939–1945), pants and casual clothing became more acceptable for women to wear, as convenience and comfort replaced strict fashion conventions.

Collection 7 Poetry   WORKSHEET **13**

SUMMER
Winslow Homer

Looking at the Painting

1. What aspects of Homer's painting capture the feeling of summer?

_____

_____

_____

_____

2. How does Homer's depiction of summer's natural beauty differ from Shakespeare's in "Shall I Compare Thee to a Summer's Day?"

_____

_____

_____

_____

3. How does Homer's portrayal of the woman in his painting compare with Shakespeare's portrayal of the love object of his sonnet?

_____

_____

_____

_____

4. Consider the **imagery** in Shakespeare's poem and in Homer's painting. Which artist better captures his subject? Cite examples from each work to support your answer.

_____

_____

_____

_____

SUMMER
Winslow Homer

ANSWER KEY

Introducing the Painting

1. Answers may vary. The woman appears to be trimming or picking flowers growing in a hanging pot.

2. The woman's head is the focal point of the painting. Our eyes are drawn to the woman's head because the relative darkness of her head is contrasted against a beige background. It is also framed by a strong vertical element (the post) and an irregular horizontal element (the wavy line of the background vegetation).

3. The light sky at the top of the painting is balanced by the dark foreground; the post, woman, and vines are strong, parallel, vertical elements and create balance.

4. Answers may vary. The artist may have been trying to convey a mood of tranquility and security since he shows the woman alone—peaceful, composed, and absorbed in her work among the beautiful plants in her garden.

5. Answers may vary. The attitude of the artist toward the woman seems to be one of admiration and respect, or at least regard for her bearing and aesthetic quality.

Looking at the Painting

1. Answers may vary. The beige, hazy sky, the lush flowering plants, and the lightly dressed (for the times) woman capture the feeling of summer.

2. Answers may vary. Homer's depiction of summer emphasizes its deep green foliage, lovely flowers, and hazy comfort, whereas Shakespeare's depiction focuses on summer's uncomfortable heat, rough winds, cloudiness, and quickly fading beauty.

3. Answers may vary. While all answers supported by reason are acceptable, most students will probably see that Homer portrays the woman figure as beautiful, poised, and refined; but Shakespeare's portrayal of the love object in his sonnet goes even further in its passionate, love-struck claim that she is more beautiful, temperate, and lasting than a summer day.

4. Answers may vary. Some students may consider the rich greens, the passionate red flowers, the lovely woman set off against the sky, and the overall lightness of Homer's soft-edged style as the more effective portrayal of summer and feminine beauty. Others may find that Shakespeare's extended comparison of his love object with summer ("Thou art more lovely and more temperate") better captures the vitality of the exalted woman ("thy eternal summer shall not fade") and the extremity of summer ("Sometimes too hot the eye of heaven shines").

EXTENSION AND ENRICHMENT

Writing Connections

1. Write a one-act play or a scene from a play in which you tell us who the woman in the painting is, what she's doing, and why. Make sure your play or scene contains an element of conflict. The play or scene will be evaluated on the basis of the following criteria:
   • The play or scene tells us about the woman's personality and develops a story about what she's doing and why.
   • The play or scene contains a conflict.
   • The play or scene is relatively free of mistakes in spelling, grammar, usage, and mechanics.

Crossing the Curriculum: Gardening

2. Find one book or more in the library or at home about gardening and different types of gardens. Based on the types of plants that grow in your area, plan your ideal garden. List the plants you will grow and the time of year you will need to plant them. Make a drawing, diagram, or painting of your ideal garden. The project will be evaluated on the basis of the following criteria:
   • The information on plants is accurate and well researched.
   • The plants you have chosen for your garden grow in your area.
   • The drawing, diagram, or painting is neat, and incorporates your research and plans for your ideal garden.

PORTRAIT OF A BOY
Egypto-Roman

Using Transparency 14

This transparency will complement the selection "Geraldo No Last Name" by Sandra Cisneros (Student Edition, Col. 8, p. 558). To complete the Looking at the Painting blackline master, students will have to read this short story. Students should also be made aware of information in About the Art. This transparency may also be used with other selections.

Introducing the Painting

1. This work was painted in encaustic, a process using a mixture of heated beeswax and pigments. Describe the colors and the style of brush strokes.

2. How does the artist create the illusion of depth?

3. Where does the light come from in the portrait, and how does the artist render the quality of the light?

4. Why do you think this boy in his young-teenage years was the subject of a funerary portrait?

5. What aspect of the portrait do you find the most striking? Do you think the work captures the boy's individuality? Explain.

Focusing on Background

About the Culture Egypto-Roman funerary portraits brought a Roman style of painting to Egyptian customers seeking these images for their journey to the afterlife. During the Roman rule of Egypt, these commissions were common. The work was displayed in the home while the subject remained alive. When the person died, the portrait would be cut down and placed over the face of the mummy, with the outermost wrapping holding it in place.

Most of the surviving portraits have been traced to the Faiyum region in northern Egypt, about seventy miles south of modern Cairo. Although Rome ruled Egypt at the time, the portraits reflect the Egyptian tradition of adorning mummies with a sculptured mask of the deceased person. In the times of the pharaohs, these images had a formulaic style, ignoring individual characteristics. Greco-Roman portraiture, with its emphasis on individual identity, changed that quality.

Portrait painting was reasonably common during the Rome Republic. The only examples that exist today, however, are the Egyptian mummy portraits, which date back to the second century A.D. While the style originated in Greece in the fifth century B.C., Roman artists refined the approach. The Egyptians who commissioned the work must have enjoyed the diverse cultures around them: the subjects of the portraits are dressed and coiffed like Romans, and many also carry Greek names or Greek versions of Egyptian names. But their families found their spiritual reassurance in long-held Egyptian beliefs.

About the Art This work, typical of Faiyum portraits, was painted in a complex technique called encaustic, in which pigments were mixed with heated beeswax and other solvents, such as egg and resin. This process enabled artists to get effects comparable to those of oil painting, which did not come about until the 1200s. The boy's head, for example, stands off from the background, lending a sense of depth. Fluid brush strokes model, or give a three-dimensional quality to, the face, as does the fine blend of light and dark pigments.

Children, of course, were not expected to die. So this portrait may have been painted quickly, after a fatal accident. Or the boy's family, expecting imminent death from illness, may have sought a likeness of his face. Someone looking only at that face now could think it was painted last week, not nineteen hundred years ago. The young teenager stares placidly at the viewer; his hair is cut short and a bit piled, giving him a contemporary look. His Roman tunic is accented by a purple clavus, or vertical stripe, on his shoulder.

Humanities Connection

History Mummification was practiced throughout most of early Egyptian history. The Egyptians probably began to intentionally mummify the dead around 2600 B.C. They continued and developed the practice for over 2,500 years, into the Roman period (30 B.C.–A.D. 364). The quality of the mummification varied, depending on the price paid. The best-preserved mummies date from the Eighteenth to Twentieth Dynasties during the New Kingdom (1570–1075 B.C.) and include Tutankhamen and other well-known pharaohs.

Collection 8 Evaluating Style • Evaluating an Argument   WORKSHEET **14**

PORTRAIT OF A BOY
Egypto-Roman

Looking at the Painting

1. Looking at this portrait, do you imagine anything about this boy who lived almost two thousand years ago? Do you think this boy had concerns or problems similar to those that you have? Explain your answer.

_____

_____

_____

_____

2. How is this ancient mummy portrait connected with the contemporary short story "Geraldo No Last Name" by Sandra Cisneros?

_____

_____

_____

_____

3. The inscription on the boy's tunic says that his name was Eutyches. Compare the artist's portrayal of Eutyches with Cisneros's prose portrayal of Geraldo.

_____

_____

_____

_____

4. Compare the mood of the portrait with the mood of Cisneros's story. How can the **aesthetic approach** explain the impact of the **style** on the mood of each work?

_____

_____

_____

_____

PORTRAIT OF A BOY
Egypto-Roman

ANSWER KEY

Introducing the Painting

1. Answers may vary. The colors, ranging from dark and light browns to olive and off-white, are rich and earthy; the style of the brush strokes ranges from smooth and flowing to fast and rough.

2. Answers may vary. The artist creates the illusion of depth by modeling the face with light effects and shadow, showing the boy's left side diminishing in three-quarter view, and using a contrasting background color.

3. Answers may vary. The light comes from the left and probably above, in view of the shadow across the boy's neck. The artist renders the quality of the light by using lighter pigments (for instance, a line of white on the nose) to portray highlights on the boy's face.

4. Answers may vary. Some students may think that the boy died unexpectedly and was quickly portrayed so that he would appear to be living, whereas others may guess that he was ill and facing death at the time that he posed.

5. Answers may vary. Most students will point to the big, dark eyes as the most striking aspect of the portrait; the boy's hairstyle or expression may be striking to others; still others may focus on how timeless the face looks. Most will agree that the work captures the boy's individuality.

Looking at the Painting

1. Some students may believe that there is too great a difference between the time and culture of this boy and their own for him to have anything in common with them. Others may come up with universal teenage problems.

2. Answers may vary. The mummy portrait is connected with Cisneros's short story in that both seek to portray a young boy or man who has recently died by showing that the deceased was an individual, a significant person.

3. Answers may vary. The artist's portrayal is an attempt to render him in realistic detail, whereas Cisneros's quickly sketches a relative stranger mostly from the point of view of a character who met him just before his death.

4. Answers may vary. The mood of the portrait, aside from the purpose for it, is fairly positive, while the mood of the story is sad and mournful. The aesthetic approach can explain the impact of the style on the mood of each work by showing how, for instance, the soft expression and deep eyes of the portrait lend it an upbeat mood, whereas the matter-of-fact tone of the story contributes to the sad mood.

EXTENSION AND ENRICHMENT

Writing Connections

1. Write an elegy or a eulogy in honor of the boy in the portrait. An elegy is a poem that laments the dead; a eulogy is a speech in memory and praise of the dead. In your elegy or eulogy, imagine friends, family, and favorite activities for the dead boy. Try to explain, with vivid description, what made the boy special. The elegy or eulogy will be evaluated on the basis of the following criteria:
   • The elegy or eulogy imagines the friends, family, and interests of the boy in the portrait.
   • It has vivid language and a suitable tone.
   • The writing is relatively free of errors in spelling, grammar, usage, and mechanics.

Crossing the Curriculum:
History / Public Speaking

2. Research what life was like in Roman Egypt in the second century A.D., and present your findings in an oral report to the class. Use the school or public library and the Internet to investigate the society's class structure, economy, politics, art and architecture, and so on. Try to find pictures that will help illustrate your presentation. The oral report will be evaluated on the basis of the following criteria:
   • The oral report is well researched and provides adequate background on life in second-century Roman Egypt.
   • It is clearly presented and uses pictures.
   • The language is relatively free of errors in grammar, usage, and pronunciation.

SOLDIER'S BACKPACK AND WEAPON
E. Kenneth Hoffman

Using Transparency 15

This transparency will complement the selection "Where Have You Gone, Charming Billy?" by Tim O'Brien (Student Edition, Col. 9, p. 620). To complete the Looking at the Photograph blackline master, students will have to read this short story. Students should also be made aware of information in About the Art. This transparency may also be used with other selections.

Introducing the Photograph

1. How does this image, without showing blood or battle, reveal the danger and hard work that a soldier faces?

2. What is suggested by the helmet atop this mound of combat equipment? How might the angle of the helmet contribute to the feeling of Hoffman's image?

3. How might the background of this picture express an idea about war?

4. Could this photograph work equally well for a pro-war movement and an anti-war movement?

5. What idea do you think Hoffman intended to communicate with this picture? Do you think this image, which is an example of photojournalism, can be called art?

Focusing on Background

About the Photographer Hoffman had his own life-defining experience when he served in Vietnam, covering the war with his camera for the U.S. Army. There was a time, however, before the war, when the future photographer had not found his visual sense.

When Hoffman landed in Vietnam in 1969, he was assigned as a lieutenant in charge of a photography detachment. He oversaw combat photographers and lab technicians as a supervisor in Pleiku. Despite his responsibilities, he continued to record the war through his own lens, and these pictures that he took are archived in the Library of Congress. But Hoffman did more than document the war for the Army. Often, he brought a poetic bent to his dangerous work, shooting to achieve succinct emotion rather than objective news gathering. As he developed an interest in the culture of Vietnam, he began taking shots of the Vietnamese people. The resulting portfolio, warm and empathetic, often finds the overlooked pain of war, such as in his shot of displaced Vietnamese boys in a resettlement camp in Pleiku.

About the Art "Check out the backpack, ammo, and weapon; I once carried a home like that on my back," Larry Ash, a Vietnam War veteran, said about this photograph. Hoffman's composed image, deadpan but poignant, instantly evokes that awful home away from home for many of the approximately 8.75 million men and women who served in Vietnam. The black-and-white shot also seems to have acquired an iconic status. In a shorthand way, it appears to stand for the more than 58,000 members of the armed forces who lost their lives while fighting an increasingly unpopular war.

Beyond the idea of the unknown fallen soldier, Hoffman captures the desolation of war without showing a drop of blood. The background is dusty, barren earth—the only growth is a weak sapling that looks quite dead; an M-16 rifle, a combat helmet, and ammunition belts are prominent in the foreground. This imagery of death poetically suggests the idea that war goes against nature. Hoffman has said, "Photography doesn't lie. It captures what people are thinking through their behavior." *As Soldier's Backpack and Weapon* shows, photography can also reveal truths when people are notably absent.

Humanities Connection

History War photography flourished during the Civil War. Most surviving photographs were taken by or under the supervision of Mathew Brady. The photographic process, long and complex, required two photographers—one to mix chemicals on a glass plate and to immerse it (in darkness) in a solution, the other to position and focus the camera. After inserting the plate in the camera and exposing it for minutes, the photographers would rush the fragile plate to a darkroom wagon for developing.

**Collection 9 Biographical and Historical Approach •
Using Primary and Secondary Sources**

SOLDIER'S BACKPACK AND WEAPON

E. Kenneth Hoffman

Looking at the Photograph

1. What idea might Hoffman's photograph communicate about the importance of the person, the individual, who fights as a soldier? Explain your answer.

_____

_____

_____

_____

2. Compare the mood of this image with the mood of Tim O'Brien's story "Where Have You Gone, Charming Billy?" Cite aspects of each work to support your answer.

_____

_____

_____

_____

3. How might Hoffman's picture evoke the irony in the title of O'Brien's story?

_____

_____

_____

_____

4. How can Hoffman's photograph and O'Brien's short story be viewed critically from the **historical approach**?

_____

_____

_____

_____

SOLDIER'S BACKPACK AND WEAPON
E. Kenneth Hoffman

ANSWER KEY

Introducing the Photograph

1. Answers may vary. The image reveals the danger a soldier faces by prominently showing the M-16 rifle and the ammunition belts of long, pointy bullets, and it reveals the mass of equipment that a soldier must carry in combat.

2. Answers may vary. The helmet suggests a person, or the specific soldier, to whom this equipment has been assigned. The angle of the helmet, pointing down, seems to contribute to the sadness of the image.

3. Answers may vary. The background, which is desolate and lifeless, might express the idea that war annihilates life or goes against nature.

4. Answers may vary. Some students may believe that the poignant absence of a soldier amid the tools of war suggests death and that the image could be used in an anti-war movement. Others may take the image more literally and see the equipment as exciting and therefore think that it could be used as pro-war propaganda.

5. Answers may vary. Some students may think that Hoffman intended merely to show the dangerous arms and heavy equipment that a soldier must carry, whereas others may think that he intended to suggest the killing and sad devastation of war. Opinions on whether or not the image can be called art should be supported by reasons.

Looking at the Photograph

1. Answers may vary. Hoffman's photograph, by showing only the equipment of war, may communicate the idea that the actual individual who fights is not important, at least not to the government that carries on the war.

2. Answers may vary. The image, showing weaponry against a barren background and suggesting a dead soldier, will strike most students as having a sad mood; the mood of O'Brien's story, with its look at Paul's fear and its grim recounting of Billy's awful fate, may be viewed as even more disturbing and gruesome.

3. Answers may vary. Hoffman's picture might evoke the irony of O'Brien's title because the equipment topped by a helmet looks like a person, but the person, like the dead Billy in O'Brien's title, is not there.

4. Answers may vary. Both Hoffman's photograph and O'Brien's short story can be viewed critically from the historical approach because both works reflect the key events of their time, namely the Vietnam War.

EXTENSION AND ENRICHMENT

Writing Connections

1. Imagine the soldier whose equipment is shown. Did he die? Was he wounded? Or is there an innocent reason that the pack is unattended? Write a short story about the soldier, using vivid description, characterization, and dialogue. Give your story a beginning, a middle, and an end. The end should feature the image of the gear, and by that point the soldier's fate should be clear. The short story will be evaluated on the basis of the following criteria:
   • The story has a beginning, a middle, and an end.
   • The story describes the imaginary soldier in vivid detail, explains his fate, and ends with Hoffman's image.
   • The story has at least one instance of dialogue.
   • The story is relatively free of errors in spelling, grammar, usage, and mechanics.

Crossing the Curriculum: History

2. Some people view this photograph as an anti-war statement. Research the peace movement during the Vietnam War. Write a two-page research paper including background on the time period. The paper will be evaluated on the basis of the following criteria:
   • The paper answers the questions mentioned above.
   • The paper includes appropriate historical background on the Vietnam War era.
   • The paper is relatively free of errors in spelling, grammar, usage, and mechanics.

Collection 9 Biographical and Historical Approach • Using Primary and Secondary Sources

CEREMONY AT SUNSET
Harold Hitchcock

Using Transparency 16

Use this transparency with "The Sword in the Stone" by Sir Thomas Malory (Student Edition, Col. 9, p. 644). To complete the Looking at the Painting blackline master, students will have to read this legend. Students should also be made aware of information in About the Art. This transparency may also be used with other selections.

Introducing the Painting

1. Describe the landscape in the painting.

2. What compass direction are the people and horses facing in the painting? How do you know?

3. What effect do the muted colors have on the scene?

4. What do you notice first in the painting? Then, where is your eye drawn? Why?

5. How does the size of the trees affect the scene?

Focusing on Background

About the Artist Harold Hitchcock was born in London in 1914. Hitchcock's father ran two thriving businesses into bankruptcy during Hitchcock's childhood, and as a result Hitchcock and his two younger siblings were sent to live with their maternal grandparents. Hitchcock's grandfather, a genteel, loving ex-schoolmaster, was a powerful influence on the sensitive boy and encouraged him to paint. One day, in his grandparents' garden, Hitchcock had a mystical vision of great beauty that filled him with a strong sense of well-being and peace. He became determined to recapture in art something of the experience. By the time he was thirteen, Hitchcock was gaining public attention for painting what became the subject of all of his art, imaginary natural landscapes.

Hitchcock, a conscientious objector in World War II (1939–1945), served in the army in a noncombatant role. After the war he worked as a commercial artist, employment that he found soul-destroying, so he abandoned it in 1964. Hitchcock changed his birth name Raymond to Harold in 1960 for religious reasons. Since leaving commercial art, Hitchcock has enjoyed success

as a painter of landscapes that, while out of step with the progression of modern art, make artistic links between humankind, nature, and spiritual awareness.

About the Art Harold Hitchcock lives in Ugborough, an ancient Saxon village in Devon, a southern county of England. Many of the stories about King Arthur and his knights are traditionally thought to have taken place in this region. After moving to Ugborough, but before knowing of its connection with Camelot, Hitchcock was inspired to paint a series of fantasy seascapes and landscapes about King Arthur and his knights of the Round Table.

Hitchcock, who paints mostly in watercolor or gouache, demonstrates his great skill and craftsmanship with the watercolor medium in *Ceremony at Sunset*. With the foreground horse, he is able to get the rich depth and controlled line of a realistic oil painting. At the same time, he deftly makes the transition to the light, soft-edged quality of watercolor in the dreamlike background of the painting. This work is typical of Hitchcock's surrealistic landscapes, which project the uplifting beauty of nature and the unique vision of the artist. Light—crystalline and pure—permeates the scene and gives it a luminous tone. And while the smoky-orange glow underscores the scene's mythical resonance, Hitchcock never forgets the source and direction of that light. The work, as a result, seems magical but oddly real.

Humanities Connection

History and Legends The town of Glastonbury, county of Somerset, in southern England, has had a long and illustrious history. Iron Age dwellings (c. 1000 B.C.), as well as Roman settlements (first century A.D.), have been excavated there. In addition, two significant legends are associated with the town. One says that the bones of King Arthur and Queen Guinevere were discovered in Glastonbury in the twelfth century and then reburied at the abbey there. The other legend states that an early Christian saint, St. Joseph of Arimathea, brought the Holy Grail, the chalice used in the Last Supper of Christ, to Glastonbury.

Collection 9 Biographical and Historical Approach • Using Primary and Secondary Sources

WORKSHEET 16

CEREMONY AT SUNSET
Harold Hitchcock
Looking at the Painting

1. What in the painting makes you think you could or could not find a hero in the scene?

_____

_____

_____

_____

2. What kind of ceremony might the painting represent? Does it remind you of any ceremony in Sir Thomas Malory's "The Sword in the Stone"?

_____

_____

_____

_____

3. How does the mood of the painting compare with the mood of the excerpt from Malory's legend?

_____

_____

_____

_____

4. Malory wrote in the 1400s, and Hitchcock painted this scene in 1977; yet both look to a magical past. How might this looking back in both works be viewed from the **historical approach**?

_____

_____

_____

_____

CEREMONY AT SUNSET
Harold Hitchcock

ANSWER KEY

Introducing the Painting

1. Answers may vary. The landscape is hilly and has a lot of vegetation, including enormous trees. It also has buildings and monuments of classical architecture and rocky outcroppings.

2. The people and horses are facing west because the name of the painting says it is sunset and the people are facing the light from the setting sun.

3. Answers may vary. The muted colors give a soft, peaceful, slightly misty look to the painting. Their soft, misty quality also gives the work a magical feeling or atmosphere.

4. Answers may vary. Many viewers will first notice the white horse and then have their eyes drawn to the center and up through the painting toward the light. The light in the painting creates such a path.

5. Answers may vary. The towering, billowing trees give a look of importance, grandeur, and mystery to the scene. They also seem to encircle the place where the ceremony takes place, in effect hiding it and making it seem more enchanted.

Looking at the Painting

1. Answers may vary. Students will probably consider knights heroic, and, because there are knights in the painting, they will probably maintain that it is a suitable setting for a traditional hero. The white horses, heraldic banner, and classical architecture also are trappings traditionally associated with western heroes.

2. Answers may vary. The ceremony in the painting might represent a coronation (ceremony of crowning a king or queen), an investiture (knighting ceremony), a dedication of a shrine, a funeral, or possibly a wedding. The coronation idea best matches Malory's legend, which ends with the scene of Arthur's coronation.

3. Answers may vary. Some students may say that both works have a magical mood, since each

features British knights from long ago. Others may think that even though Malory's tale includes Arthur's predestiny as king and the magic sword in the stone, its straightforward style is not as magical as Hitchcock's painting, which depicts a mystical light and a solemn ceremony in an idyllic location.

4. Answers may vary. The looking back in "The Sword in the Stone" can be seen from the historical approach because the feudal order had broken down in England, and the nation's political and social life were in turmoil. The historical approach may apply to Hitchcock's looking back because his period also featured turmoil, such as wars (World War II and the Vietnam War), social upheaval, and economic difficulties.

EXTENSION AND ENRICHMENT

Writing Connections

1. Imagine that you are attending the ceremony shown in the painting. Write a letter to a friend describing your experience, telling what you wore, where you stood, what you did, and of what the ceremony consisted. The letter will be evaluated on the basis of the following criteria:
   • The letter is in personal letter form.
   • The letter describes what you wore and what took place at the ceremony in the painting.
   • The letter is relatively free of errors in spelling, grammar, usage, and mechanics.

Crossing the Curriculum: Art History

2. Find an art book that includes surrealist art. Pick out your favorite painting and show it to your class. Be prepared to tell who the artist is, what appeals to you about the painting, and why you preferred it to the other art in the book. The presentation will be evaluated on the basis of the following criteria:
   • The art was chosen from a book of surrealist art.
   • The presentation includes the name of the artist, your opinion of the art, and why it appeals to you more than the other art in the book.

DEATH OF MARAT
Jacques Louis David

Using Transparency 17

This transparency will complement the selection *The Tragedy of Julius Caesar* by William Shakespeare (Student Edition, Col. 10, p. 754). To complete the Looking at the Painting blackline master, students will have to read this play. Students should also be made aware of information in About the Art. This transparency may also be used with other selections.

Introducing the Painting

1. What are the predominant colors in this painting? What effect does the palette produce?

2. What direction does the light come from, and how does David use it to direct the viewer's attention?

3. How does the artist make Marat look heroic?

4. Why do you think David included Marat's patched sheet and the crate that he used as a table?

5. What do you think David wanted viewers to feel when they look at this portrait? Explain your answer.

Focusing on Background

About the Artist Jacques Louis David (1748–1825) emerged from the Reign of Terror with blood on his hands. A zealot of the French Revolution (1789–1799) and friend of its notorious leader Robespierre, he rose to the Committee of General Security in 1793. In that role he sent three hundred people to the guillotine.

David was born into a prosperous bourgeois family in Paris. But when he was just nine, the family was shattered: His father was killed, and his mother left him with his uncles. As for school, David said, "I was always . . . drawing for the duration of the class." This behavior paid off. At sixteen, he began studying art at the Académie Royale under the rococo painter J. M. Vien. Though clearly talented, he toiled obscurely in frilly rococo style through his twenties. In 1774, however, David won the coveted Prix de Rome, and on the awarded trip to Italy, he became enamored of classical art. The work of the painter Nicolas Poussin (1594–1665), itself classically inspired, also proved influential. In

a seismic shift, David, who spent six years in Rome, found his own neoclassical style.

Despite shifting to realism after 1789 to record the revolution, David used his heroic tone for preferred figures, as *Death of Marat,* makes clear. Then, events changed. Jailed for his role in the Reign of Terror, he was later released at the behest of his wife and students. In 1797, again at the center stage of France, David met Napoleon Bonaparte, and from 1799 to 1815, he was his official painter. After Napoleon's downfall in 1815, David was exiled to Brussels in what is now Belgium, where he took on Greco-Roman mythological subjects until his death.

About the Art A sharp orator and bosom friend of Robespierre, Jean Paul Marat was seen as a patriot by some, a brutal demagogue by others. On July 13, 1793, Charlotte Corday, a young Royalist with a wily ruse about a petition, gained entry to his apartment. Finding Marat in his tub, where he habitually sat for hours treating a disfiguring skin disease, Corday stabbed him to death.

David, a colleague and friend, saw Marat as a model of virtue and simplicity. Officially invited to do Marat's portrait, David arrived a day after the murder, only to find that the body's decomposed state had made lifelike depiction impossible. So the effects of time and summer heat, coupled with David's emotional state, resulted in this idealized image. The face, softly lit, is peaceful. Conversely, David throws harsh light on the murderer's petition, which he added to the scene (along with the bloody knife) to show the assassin's treachery.

Humanities Connection

History David was a visual cheerleader for the French Revolution. His majestic historical paintings, such as *Death of Socrates* and *Brutus's Sons,* were hailed as artistic calls for political action. He planned the Festival of the People on July 14, 1790, which celebrated the storming of the Bastille, an infamous prison, in the previous year (and continues today as Bastille Day, a holiday in France). Also, in addition to designing banners, triumphal arches, and inspirational props, David voted to behead King Louis XVI.

Collection 10 Drama • Evaluating an Argument

DEATH OF MARAT
Jacques Louis David

Looking at the Painting

1. Is this painting primarily a propaganda image of a political ally or a heartfelt portrait of a murdered friend? Explain your answer.

_____

_____

_____

_____

2. Consider David's relationship with Marat. What **characters** from William Shakespeare's *The Tragedy of Julius Caesar* do they parallel? Why?

_____

_____

_____

_____

3. Compare the techniques that David and Shakespeare use to heighten the drama of the real-life assassinations that they portray. (Think of weapons, blood, and so on.)

_____

_____

_____

_____

4. This painting portrays an assassination from a certain viewpoint. What speech in Shakespeare's play is it connected with? Why is it a visual parallel to that **dramatic** speech?

_____

_____

_____

_____

DEATH OF MARAT
Jacques Louis David

ANSWER KEY

Introducing the Painting

1. Answers may vary. The predominant colors in the painting are dark brown or umber (reddish brown), middle-tone to dark green, off-white, and light yellowish browns. The palette produces an earthy effect and a sad feeling.

2. Answers may vary. The light comes from the left and above (from a window, perhaps), and the artist uses shadow and contrast to direct the viewer's attention to Marat's face, the assassin's petition, and the crate that bears David's dedication ("To Marat, David").

3. Answers may vary. David makes Marat look heroic by using dramatic lighting and by echoing classical portrayals of the descent of Christ from the cross and the lamentation of Mary over his body, including Michelangelo's *Pietà,* in Marat's posture.

4. Answers may vary. David probably included the patched sheet and crate to demonstrate what he viewed as Marat's simple and virtuous poverty, which was in contrast to the wealth of France's corrupt royalty.

5. Answers may vary. David wanted viewers to feel sorrow and indignation over the brutal assassination of a great man, along with the treachery and duplicity of the assassin and perhaps, by extension, that of all Royalists.

Looking at the Painting

1. Answers may vary. Some students will see the image as propaganda, since David did not portray Marat objectively; others will think that it is a sincerely emotional portrait of a slain friend. Either view is acceptable if supported by reasons.

2. Answers may vary. David's relationship with Marat, a friend and political ally, most closely resembles the one between Caesar and Antony in that Caesar, like Marat, was slain, and Antony, like David, was outraged.

3. Answers may vary. David uses lighting, Marat's posture, and the bloody petition and knife to heighten the drama of Marat's assassination.

Shakespeare uses the ruse of the appeal for Publius Cimber, the stabbing by the various assassins, Caesar's line "Et tu, Brutè?," and the dipping of the assassins' hands in Caesar's blood to dramatize Caesar's assassination.

4. Answers may vary. The painting is connected with Antony's speech to the crowd in Act III, Scene 2, in that both seek to persuade an audience of the treachery of the assassin(s) and the virtues and honor of the assassinated leader.

EXTENSION AND ENRICHMENT

Writing Connections

1. Imagine the assassin, Charlotte Corday, who killed Marat. Why did she do it? What kind of man was Marat? Do some research on the topic, and then create a poem written from Corday's point of view. The poem should relate her motive and her emotions up through the moment when she stabs Marat. The poem will be evaluated on the basis of the following criteria:
   - The poem is written from Corday's point of view.
   - The poem relates Corday's motive and emotions.
   - The poem is relatively free of errors in spelling, grammar, usage, and mechanics.

Crossing the Curriculum: History

2. The artist who created this painting acted from fiercely held political views. Research Jacques Louis David, and write a two-page paper on his role in the French Revolution. What ended David's involvement with the revolution? Be sure to include the relationship between David's artistic values and his political beliefs. The research paper will be evaluated on the basis of the following criteria:
   - The paper offers sufficient background on the French Revolution and the Reign of Terror.
   - The paper explains David's role in the revolution and the connection between his artistic and political values.
   - The paper is relatively free of errors in spelling, grammar, usage, and mechanics.